YORK NOTES

General Editors: Professor A.N. Jeffares (~~University~~
of Stirling) & Professor Suheil Bushrui (~~American~~
University of Beirut)

Geoffrey Chaucer

PROLOGUE TO THE CANTERBURY TALES

Notes by Michael Alexander

MA (OXFORD)
*Senior Lecturer, Department of English Studies,
University of Stirling*

LONGMAN
YORK PRESS

YORK PRESS
Immeuble Esseily, Place Riad Solh, Beirut.

LONGMAN GROUP LIMITED
Longman House, Burnt Mill,
Harlow, Essex CM20 2JE, England
and Associated Companies throughout the World.

© Librairie du Liban 1980

First published 1980
Second impression 1984
ISBN 0 582 78228 7

Printed in Hong Kong by
Sheck Wah Tong Printing Press Ltd

Contents

Part 1

Introduction

Chaucer's life

Geoffrey Chaucer came from a middle-class family which rose in the world through four successive generations. The Chaucers were originally from France; *chaussier* means 'shoemaker'. Geoffrey's grandfather was a wine-merchant importing from France. Geoffrey's father, John, was also a wine-merchant in the Vintry in London, where the poet was born in the early 1340s. John once held minor court office as Butler, and Geoffrey followed him in his career as a royal servant. Geoffrey had a sister (or daughter) who became a nun. Curiously, both his mother and his father's mother were married three times.

Geoffrey was made a page to Prince Lionel, Edward III's third son. In his teens he fought in the English army in France, where he was captured; Edward III ransomed him in 1360. Little is known of him then until he is recorded as being in Spain in 1366, a year in which he married Philippa Payne Roet, a sister of Katherine Swynford, the mistress and later the wife of John of Gaunt, Edward III's fifth son. In 1367 he began travelling abroad on the King's business. In 1369 he fought in Picardy for John of Gaunt. In 1372 he went to Genoa and Florence on a diplomatic mission, and revisited Italy in 1378 on a mission to the Lord of Milan.

From 1374 Chaucer's career is well documented, for he became Controller of Customs and Subsidy of Wools, Skins and Hides, England's largest trade. He bought a house over Aldgate, the east gate of the City of London. In 1377 he was allowed a Deputy at the Custom House and moved to Kent, which he represented in Parliament for three years, and was also a Justice of the Peace. Once more in favour, he was Clerk for the King's Works in 1389-90, but retired from his busy public life after being robbed and beaten two or three times in four days.

In his last decade, Chaucer was a royal pensioner and substitute forester of the royal forest of North Petherton in Somerset, an office in which he was confirmed by Henry IV in 1399. In 1400 he took a lease on a house in the garden of Westminster Abbey, but died on 25 October and was buried in a chapel of the Abbey which has since become Poets' Corner.

Literary career

English poetry flowered in the reign of Richard II after nearly three centuries' submergence beneath the prevailing French tradition. *Piers Plowman*, by William Langland (*c*.1331–99?), and the anonymous *Sir Gawain and the Green Knight* are composed in alliterative metres deriving from Old English verse. Chaucer's metre and technique, however, derive from the Romance languages. He wrote only in English, unlike John Gower (?1330–1408), a court poet ten years his senior, who wrote in French and Latin also. Thus, although he had competent predecessors and, in Langland and the author of *Gawain*, two great contemporaries, Chaucer is recognised as the father of English poetry.

Chaucer's work falls into what have been called his French, Italian and English periods. Before 1378 he was heavily influenced by French traditions. He translated some of the famous *Roman de la Rose* and wrote *The Book of the Duchess* (1369), his first original work, in imitation of French allegorical dream-vision poems. His later dream-visions (*The House of Fame* and *The Parliament of Fowls*) are increasingly influenced by Italian models, and the latter, a mature piece, is the best of his minor poems. Some of the early tales belong to the French period, such as the Life of St Cecilia and the stories of Constance and Griselda.

Chaucer's second visit to Italy in 1378 opened his eyes to a much richer tradition in the work of Dante (1275–1321), whose *Commedia* he echoes many times, and Boccaccio (1313–75) whose *Teseida* and *Filostrato* became Chaucer's *Knight's Tale* and *Troilus and Criseyde*, both among his greatest poems. In these years he also translated the *Consolation of Philosophy* of Boethius (into prose) and began *The Legend of Good Women*, his last work in the French tradition; like several of his works, it remained unfinished.

The Canterbury Tales were probably conceived in 1385, when Chaucer went into Kent. The loose narrative framework enabled him to find room for some of his old stories, and to develop his dramatic and realistic abilities. This last phase, the 'English period', contains Chaucer's most vigorous and artistically mature work. But Chaucer was a Catholic and a European as well as an English poet, and the earlier influences are present also in the later work, though it is more fully his own and more fully expresses both his humour and the life of his time. It should not be forgotten that the pentameter line, which he naturalised so completely in English, came from France. Chaucer is the first European writer to write in English and he gives us a sane, civilised and inclusive view of his world and of human life as a whole.

In Chaucer's large body of work, several traditions meet—popular, learned and courtly. He was a court poet, but as close to his audience as any popular entertainer. His formal education must have been rhetorical; he was full of French and Italian poetry; and he had scientific and philosophical interests: yet his English is always rapid, clear, unaffected and natural. Edmund Spenser, who recreated the English poetic tradition, called Chaucer a 'well of English undefyled'.

Chaucer's world

Born into the emergent middle class, Chaucer's public experience of life was through various offices of the royal court, though he was a government servant rather than a courtier. England passed through a profound change during his lifetime. In Chaucer's childhood, England, having beaten the Scots and the French in war, was at the peak of her prestige, with the victories of Crécy (1346) and Poitiers (1356). In 1349 Edward III founded the Order of the Garter, the supreme Order of Western chivalry. In 1360 France ceded much territory to England.

However, the Black Death of 1349 had killed a third of the people of England, and returned again in the 1360s. The resultant labour shortage disrupted the feudal economy. Edward III's costly war policy began to fail, and in old age the King became unpopular. Richard II came to the throne as a child in 1377, in a time of social unrest which broke out in the Peasants' Revolt in 1381, when John of Gaunt's palace was sacked and Archbishop Sudbury murdered in the street. There was also religious controversy: the Popes had been in captivity at Avignon since 1305, and in 1378 the Great Schism began, when rival claimants disputed the Papacy. The Oxford reformer, Wyclif, attacked Church abuses in the 1370s, and even criticised Church dogma. Little of this unrest gets into Chaucer's work, realistic as it is. He sees clearly the greed of the new bourgeoisie and the abuses in the Church, but his values are traditional. He seems entirely orthodox in religion and in politics; he was certainly discreet, as befits a diplomat and a royal servant.

Chaucer's humorous portrait of himself in *The Canterbury Tales* gives nothing away. The Host calls upon him to tell a tale,

And seyde thus: 'What man artow?'* quod he;
'Thou lookest as thou woldest fynde an hare,
For evere upon the ground I se thee stare.

Approche neer, and looke up murily.
Now war yow, sires, and lat this man have place!
He in the waast is shape as wel as I;

---

* **artow:** art thou; **quod:** said; **woldest:** wouldst; **war yow, sires:** pay attention, gentlemen; **waast:** waist. The Host, who is stout, is having a joke at the expense of Chaucer, who is also stout.

This were a popet in an arm t'enbrace
For any womman, smal and fair of face.
He semeth elvyssh by his contenaunce,
For unto no wight dooth he daliaunce.'

Chaucer flourished quietly at Richard II's court, where English medieval civilisation had its last great period before the chaos of the Wars of the Roses in the fifteenth century. Nor did Henry IV, John of Gaunt's son, reject his father's old follower when he took the throne. Richard was deposed in 1399 and murdered in 1400. Shakespeare's history plays show Richard as the last of the medieval kings; the Chaucerian synthesis was no longer to be possible.

The social and intellectual structure of Chaucer's world was clearly hierarchical (see page 47), and its social and intellectual distinctions had legal force. The old feudal system, where social standing was determined by the amount of land a man held from the king, was giving way to a more open and mercantile economic pattern, especially in London, where Chaucer came from the merchant class. He was not a man of the people, but his origins were equally remote from the nobility: there are no serfs or barons among his pilgrims. His career gave him a wide experience of English life, and especially the life of London, many of whose thirty thousand inhabitants he must have known. Medieval society, in spite of or perhaps because of its vertical distinctions, was also communal and organic: each of Chaucer's pilgrims, however individual, is conceived of as typical of his craft or profession, and as having a place in society.

The ascendancy of the Christian Church over men's minds is what most clearly differentiates Chaucer's England from that of today. An agreed theological understanding of life governed the interpretation put upon every physical and moral event, however material or secular its nature—whether meteorological, psychological or personal. Europe, or Christendom, was throughout a Catholic community, whose language was Latin. There was the same Church in every country and the same Christian social and spiritual ideal—however different its local manifestations and however corrupt or incomplete its realisation. There was as yet no alternative, secular vision of life. The integration of social, religious and cultural ideals is what allows Chaucer's work its unified simplicity and wide scope.

* **popet:** doll; **t'enbrace:** to embrace; **smal . . . face:** slender and with an attractive face (refers to Chaucer, not the woman); **elvyssh:** elvish, like an elf; **contenaunce:** countenance, facial expression; **dooth he daliaunce:** does he pay court.

A note on the text

The Canterbury Tales survive in some ninety manuscripts, which give different parts of the tales in different orders, and have all sorts of variant readings. However, the text of the *General Prologue* is not greatly in dispute. This commentary is based on the text of F.N. Robinson, *The Complete Works of Geoffrey Chaucer*, second edition, Oxford University Press, London, 1957.

Part 2

Summaries
of THE GENERAL PROLOGUE TO
THE CANTERBURY TALES

A general summary

In the *General Prologue*, Chaucer tells how, at the Tabard Inn in Southwark on the night before his pilgrimage to the shrine of Thomas à Becket in Canterbury, he fell in with a company of twenty-nine pilgrims. At the suggestion of the Host of the Tabard, they agree to tell two tales on the way to Canterbury and two on the way back to London, and the best tale is to earn its teller a free supper at the Tabard on their return. The pilgrims accept the Host as judge of the tale-telling game.

When they set out next morning, the pilgrims draw lots to decide who shall tell the first tale, and the Knight wins. His noble tale of Palamon and Arcite is admired, particularly by the nobler pilgrims, and the Host invites the Monk, as senior churchman, to tell the next tale. However, the Miller, who is already drunk, insists instead on telling a bawdy story about the cuckolding of a carpenter; and the Reeve, who is also a carpenter, angrily answers with a bawdier story about a miller. The Cook then begins on a still bawdier tale of an apprentice and a prostitute, but the first Fragment of the *Tales* ends when the Cook has scarcely begun.

This pattern of solemnity followed by comic and even ribald chaos is echoed in more than one of the remaining nine fragments of the *Tales*, in which twenty-two more pilgrims tell their very varied tales, including Chaucer himself (who tells two) and the Parson, whose tale, a long treatise on Christian penitence, ends the collection. *The Canterbury Tales* thus comes to an end before Canterbury is reached, and before the tale-telling competition has completed the first of its four stages.

The Canterbury Tales, then, is an incomplete work, perhaps because of the poet's death, although many of his works are unfinished. However, the design of the work is clear enough. As in other medieval collections of popular story, such as the Arabian *Thousand and One Nights* or the *Decameron*, by Chaucer's contemporary, Boccaccio, the primary story forms a convenient framework to a miscellany of many different kinds of tales: romances, fairy-stories, bawdy tales, sermons, saints' lives, beast-fables, allegories. However, this frame-story, as it is sometimes called, has a life of its own. Some of the tales are dramatic expressions of the characters of their tellers, and the events of the pilgrimage are sometimes of greater interest and significance than the tales. Finally, many critics see the pilgrimage itself as having a symbolic significance which gives the work its underlying purpose.

The *General Prologue* (so called to differentiate it from prologues to individual tales) is the general narrative introduction to *The Canterbury Tales* as a whole. It sets the scene in spring, the season of pilgrimages, and introduces Chaucer as a pilgrim at the Tabard Inn. Then follows the series of portraits of individual pilgrims, from the Knight down to the Pardoner. Finally we meet the Host and hear his proposal for the tale-telling competition. The next morning the pilgrimage sets out, with the Knight about to begin his tale.

Detailed summaries

Introduction: Exordium (lines 1–18)

In spring, when flowers grow and birds sing, people long to go on pilgrimage, and the English particularly love to go to Canterbury, the shrine of St Thomas à Becket.

NOTES AND GLOSSARY:

soote:	sweet
veyne:	vein, vessel of sap
swich . . .vertu:	a liquid such that by its power
flour:	flower
Zephirus:	god of the West Wind
eek:	also
holt:	wood
yonge:	the year is here thought of as beginning on 25 March
croppes:	the growth of leaf on trees and bushes (*not* crops like wheat and barley)
halve cours:	probably the second half of its course (in Aries)
foweles:	birds
ye:	eye
So . . . corages:	so much does Nature prick them in their hearts
palmeres:	pilgrims (those going to Jerusalem wore a palm)
straunge strondes:	foreign shores
ferne . . . londes:	remote shrines known in various lands
shires ende:	the end of every county
wende:	make their way
seke:	seek
holpen:	helped
seeke:	sick. A canonised saint can intercede with God for sick people who pray to him

blisful martir:	blessed martyr. Thomas à Becket died as a witness to the Christian faith in 1170, put to death in Canterbury Cathedral by knights of Henry II of England. Becket had been Chancellor, but when he became Archbishop of Canterbury, the supreme appointment of the Church in England, he defended the Church against the King. Canterbury, two days' ride from London into Kent, immediately became one of the chief places of pilgrimage in Europe

---

Introduction: at the Tabard (lines 19–42)

Chaucer joins a company of pilgrims staying at the same inn as himself. He describes them, in order.

NOTES AND GLOSSARY:

Bifil:	it happened, befell
Southwerk:	the suburb on the south bank of the Thames opposite the City of London
Tabard:	short armorial coat (here the name of the inn)
as I lay:	while I was staying
wide:	spacious
esed:	accommodated
shortly:	in short
hem everichon:	every one of them
anon:	presently
forward:	foreword, agreement
erly for to ryse:	to rise early
ther . . . devyse:	in the way I shall recount to you
Er that:	before
Me thynketh it:	it seems to me
condicioun:	state of being (both social and personal)
which:	of what occupation
degree:	social rank

The portraits of the pilgrims: the Knight (lines 43–78)

This devout example of Christian chivalry and of all the virtues of the military gentleman has fought honourably both for his temporal lord and for the Lord of all Christians, campaigning along the whole length of the frontier between Christendom and *hethenesse*, from Southern Spain right round the southern and eastern Mediterranean and even in Russia. Despite his prowess and his undefeated record, he was humble and courteous—a true, perfect, noble knight (72).* He offers thanks for his safe return from campaign by going on pilgrimage.

NOTES AND GLOSSARY:

worthy:	of proven valour and virtue
riden out:	go on campaign
Trouthe:	integrity, fidelity to one's obligations
fredom:	noble generosity
curteisie:	courteous conduct
therto:	moreover
ferre:	further
As wel . . . hethenesse:	not only in Christian but also in non-Christian domains
Alisaundre:	Alexandria, taken by Christian knights in 1365
Ful . . . bigonne:	many a time had he taken the head of the table (the place of honour)
Pruce:	Prussia
Lettow:	Lithuania
reysed:	campaigned
Ruce:	Russia
Gernade:	Granada, in Moorish Spain
Algezir:	Algeciras, taken in 1344
Belmarye:	Benmarin, in southern Morocco
Lyeys:	Ayas, in Turkey
Satalye:	Attalia, in Armenia
Whan:	when (1367 and 1361 respectively)
Grete See:	Mediterranean
armee:	armed expedition
Tramyssene:	Tlemcen, Western Algeria
oure feith:	Christianity
listes:	in a tournament (as in the *Knight's Tale*)
Palatye:	Balat, Turkey
Agayn:	against
prys:	reputation, esteem
worthy:	brave
wys:	wise, discreet
port:	bearing
vileynye:	rudeness
maner wight:	kind of person
verray:	true (*not* very)
gentil:	noble
hors were:	horses were

*numbers in parentheses refer to line numbers.

fustian:	coarse cotton cloth
gypon:	tunic
bismotered:	marked and spotted (with rust)
habergeon:	hauberk, coat of mail
late:	recently
viage:	campaign

The Squire (lines 79–100)

The Knight's son is an Esquire, or candidate for knighthood. He also has fought well, across the English Channel, but in the hope of winning his lady's favour. He is a *lovyere*, full of youth, gaiety and all the qualities of the spring. He also has all the requisite courtly accomplishments, and treats his father with honour.

NOTES AND GLOSSARY:

lusty:	zestful (*not* lustful)
bacheler:	probationer for the honour of knighthood (the candidate had to win his spurs by passing military and religious tests)
lokkes . . . presse:	locks as curly as if they had been set artificially
delyvere:	agile
chyvachie:	cavalry expedition
In . . . Pycardie:	Flanders, Artois and Picardy are in what is now southern Belgium and northern France—provinces claimed by England in its Hundred Years War with France
Embrouded:	embroidered (of his clothing rather than his face)
meede:	meadow
floytynge:	whistling (*or* playing the flute)
koude:	knew how to
endite:	compose words to songs
Juste:	joust (in a tournament)
purtreye:	portray, draw
hoote:	hotly
nyghtertale:	night-time
nyghtyngale:	the bird of love (compare line 11)
carf:	carved (the meat): one of the duties of an Esquire

The Yeoman (lines 101–17)

Completing the military trio, the Knight's only follower is a yeoman, or small landholder. (The Knight's yeoman probably held his land from the Knight as his feudal overlord; in turn, he was obliged to follow the Knight to war.) He is a forester by calling, as his *takel* shows, and had perhaps been an archer in the French wars. He also wears a medal of St Christopher, the patron saint of foresters.

NOTES AND GLOSSARY:

him liste:	it pleased him
he:	the yeoman
pecok:	peacock; the arrows were trimmed with peacock feathers to facilitate flight
not:	nut—that is, hair cropped short
bracer:	archer's arm-guard
harneised:	mounted
bawdryk:	baldric, belt

The Prioress (lines 118–62)

The Prioress, the head of a Priory of nuns, is thus senior to the Monk. She is a fashionable lady as well as a nun; her little dogs, for example, are forbidden by the rules of convent life.

NOTES AND GLOSSARY:

Nonne:	nun, a religious woman vowed to poverty, chastity and obedience
coy:	quiet
but:	only
Eglentyne:	a name from romances (French for sweetbriar)
service dyvyne:	divine worship (the regular church liturgy)
fetisly:	gracefully
Stratford:	Stratford-Bow, Bromley, Middlesex (*not* Stratford-upon-Avon), where there was a Benedictine convent known to Chaucer. The Prioress's French was not Parisian, though this may not be a criticism
At mete:	at table (*not* meat)
kepe:	take care
curteisie:	courtly behaviour
lest:	delight
coppe:	cup
ferthyng:	spot
after ... raughte:	reached for her food
sikerly:	certainly
of greet desport:	the gayest company
of port:	in her bearing
peyned hire:	took pains
countrefete cheere:	imitate the manner

estatlich:	dignified
to ben . . . reverence: to be esteemed worthy of respect	
for to speken:	to speak
conscience:	conscience, but also sensibility
pitous:	pitying, soft-hearted
bledde:	was bleeding
Of smale houndes: some little dogs	
flesshe:	meat
wastel-breed:	cake (French *gâteau*), or fine bread
soore:	sorely
men:	someone (an impersonal construction, like 'one')
with a yerde smerte: sharply with a stick	
wympul:	wimple, a nun's prescribed neck-covering
pynched:	fluted
tretys:	well formed
thereto:	moreover
spanne:	distance between outstretched finger and thumb
hardily:	scarcely
fetys:	well made
was war:	noticed
Smal:	slender
peire of bedes:	set of beads, used for saying the Rosary, a sequence of prayers to the Virgin Mary
gauded:	embellished. (Every eleventh bead stands for an Our Father, and is larger than the other beads, which stand for Hail Marys; these larger beads were called *gauds*.)
sheene:	beautiful
write:	engraved, cut
crowned A:	a capital A (for Latin *Amor*) surmounted by a crown
'Amor vincit omnia': 'Love conquers all'. Charity is the supreme Christian virtue	
chapeleyne:	assistant (*not* chaplain)

The Monk (lines 165–207)

The senior male cleric present is a monk, whose religious vows were the same as those of the Nun. Monks, however, were often caricatured as too fond of hunting and good living.

NOTES AND GLOSSARY:

a fair:	a good one
for the maistrie:	above all others, extremely

outridere:	estates bursar, whose duties involved riding about
venerie:	hunting (also, maybe, the pursuit of Venus)
to been . . . able:	worthy to have been head of an abbey
deyntee:	fine
Gynglen:	to jingle (bells on the bridle were fashionable)
Ther . . . celle:	In the places where this lord [*dominus* is a monk's title] was supervisor of a lesser monastery
reule:	monastic Rule. The Rule of St Benedict (or Benet) of Norcia (480–547) was the foundation of Western monasticism. St Maurus was Benedict's disciple
somdel streit:	rather strict
ilke:	same
leet . . . pace:	allowed old things [such as Rules] to pass away
heeld . . . space:	observed the freedom of modern times
gaf:	gave
pulled hen:	plucked hen (a worthless object)
hunters . . . men:	a traditional comment on such biblical figures as Esau
recheless:	careless (of his duty)
waterless:	out of water. (It was held that a monk out of his monastery is like a fish out of water.)
cloistre:	cloister, monastery
What:	why
wood:	mad
poure:	stare
swynken:	toil
Austin:	St Augustine of Hippo (354–430), Doctor of the Church, who *bit* (bid, commanded) that the religious should do manual work
served:	served, serviced; clerics were often administrators in the world
Lat . . . reserved!:	Let Austin keep his hard work to himself
he:	the monk
prikasour:	mounted hunter who follows the hare by its 'pricks', or spoor
lust:	pleasure
cost:	expense
seigh:	saw
purfiled:	trimmed at the edge
grys:	a grey fur
festne:	fasten
Ywroght:	wrought, made
curious:	remarkable
love-knot:	device

gretter:	larger
balled:	bald
as . . . enoynt:	as if he had been anointed (which, of course, he had when he became a monk)
point:	physical condition
stepe:	prominent
heed:	head
as . . . leed:	like the fire under a cauldron
prelaat:	senior cleric
forpyned:	wasted by suffering
roost:	roast meat
palfrey:	horse
berye:	berry

The Friar (lines 208–69)

A Friar (Latin *frater*, brother) though a member of a religious community is not bound to a monastic life of prayer, but preaches the gospel out in the world, living off charity. The friars were widely considered to abuse the freedom given them as mendicants and travellers, and were satirised for the faults exemplified in this pilgrim.

NOTES AND GLOSSARY:

wantowne:	lively
lymytour:	licensed to beg within a limited district
solempne:	festive
orders four:	(*i*) the Franciscans or Friars Minor, founded by St Francis of Assisi in 1210, known as the Grey Friars; (*ii*) the Dominicans, or Order of Preachers, founded by St Dominic in 1216, known as the Black Friars; (*iii*) the Carmelites, or White Friars; (*iv*) the Austin Friars (see note on page 17)
kan:	knows
daliaunce:	flirtatious flattery
maad:	arranged
cost:	expense
post:	pillar, support (see Galatians 2:9). Possibly also an obscene quibble—the young women had to get married because they were pregnant
famulier:	intimately
frankeleyns:	franklins, who were often hospitable householders
over:	above
contree:	district
worthy:	prosperous

confessioun:	the Sacrament of Confession, or Penance. Since the previous century, every Christian had been required to confess his sins once a year privately to a priest. If truly contrite, the penitent is absolved of his sins. The Friar claims to have been empowered to absolve certain sins that the *curat* (219), a secular priest, had to refer to his bishop for absolution
licenciat:	licensed to hear confessions
yeve penaunce:	give a penance. (A penance is a token punishment for sin awarded after confession, as a condition of absolution. Medieval penances were often physical: a pilgrimage was a common form of penance.)
Ther as:	in cases where
wiste:	hoped
pitaunce:	charitable donation
povre:	All four Orders were vowed to poverty
yshrive:	shriven, absolved of sin
he:	the penitent
he . . . avaunt:	the friar dared assert
He wiste:	he knew
repentaunt:	truly penitent (a prerequisite to absolution)
He . . . smerte:	He is not able to weep, although he is deeply pained. (The sincere penitent was expected to weep; the friar accepts money instead.)
preyeres:	prayers (imposed as a penance)
moote:	are able
typet . . . farsed:	cape was always stuffed
wyves:	women
murye note:	merry singing voice
koude:	knew how to
yeddynges:	popular songs retelling a romance
bar . . . pris:	took the prize outright
flour-de-lys:	lily
hostiller:	innkeeper
tappestere:	a female tapster, barmaid
bet:	better
lazar:	leper (after Lazarus)
beggestere:	begging woman (whom a friar should care for)
accorded:	suited
facultee:	official position
honest:	respectable
avaunce:	be advantageous
swich poraille:	such a poor class of people
riche:	rich people

vitaille:	victuals
over:	above
ther as:	wherever
lowely of servyse:	humble in offering his services
ferme:	rent
graunt:	licence (to beg in that district)
haunt:	home territory
sho:	shoe (a worthless object)
'In principio':	(*Latin*) 'in the beginning' (the opening words of St John's Gospel, and a favourite greeting of mendicant friars)
ferthyng:	farthing, the fourth part of a penny
er:	before
His purchas . . . rente:	His pickings were much better than his official income
rage:	play about
as . . . whelp:	just as if he were a pup
love-dayes:	days fixed for settling disputes out of court, often by the arbitration of the clergy
cloysterer:	one who lives in a cloister (like a monk, as opposed to one who lives in the world)
cope:	a priest's vestment
scoler:	student (like the Clerk in 290)
maister:	Master of Arts, a dignified title not unlike the modern Doctor of Divinity
pope:	the Pope, head of the Church
double worstede:	extra-thick woven woollen cloth
semycope:	a short cape
rounded . . . presse:	curved out like a bell from the mould (in the bell-foundry)
lipsed:	lisped
wantownesse:	self-indulgence
aryght:	truly
doon:	do
sterres:	stars
cleped:	called

The Merchant (lines 270–84)

The Merchant is the first of the non-military laymen, and the first bourgeois pilgrim, probably a member of the Merchants Adventurers or the Merchants of the Staple, the two prosperous merchant guilds of the City of London who ran the trade between England and the Low Countries, especially the export of English cloth—a trade with which

Chaucer would have been concerned in his work as a customs officer. City merchants tended to be regarded with suspicion, as newly rich financiers (notably to the Crown). The Merchant is so discreet that Chaucer does not know his name.

NOTES AND GLOSSARY:

forked berd:	forked beard, a bourgeois style
mottelee:	cloth woven with a parti-coloured figured design; perhaps the livery of the guild
hye:	high (in a high saddle)
Flaundryssh:	Flemish
bever:	beaver (fur)
resons:	opinions
solempnely:	impressively
sownynge:	proclaiming
encrees:	increase
wynnyng:	profit
He wolde . . . any thyng:	He wanted the sea to be guarded against all hazards
Middelburgh:	the Staple port on the island of Walcheren in the Netherlands; across the North Sea from Orwell, near Ipswich, Suffolk
sheeldes:	*écus*, French coins with a shield on one side. The Merchant traded in currency, which the Church considered tantamount to usury
bisette:	employed
wiste:	knew
wight:	creature
estatly:	dignified
governaunce:	conduct
chevyssaunce:	borrowing money
For sothe:	forsooth, truly
with alle:	after all
noot:	know not

The Clerk (lines 285–308)

The Clerk is a model university student, reading for a career in the Church. He is in minor orders.

NOTES AND GLOSSARY:

Oxenford:	Oxford (literally, the ford of the oxen), seat of England's senior university, founded before 1200; already famous for its logicians

logyk:	logic, the principal subject in an Arts course
ygo:	gone
leene:	lean
And he . . . undertake:	And the clerk himself was not very fat, I swear
holwe:	hollow
sobrely:	gravely
overeste:	topmost
courtepy:	short cape
geten him:	got himself
benefice:	benefice, living, post as a parish priest
office:	secular employment (usually administrative)
him . . . have:	he would rather have
heed:	side
Twenty:	a large number of manuscripts
blak or reed:	calf or sheepskin
Aristotle:	the Greek philosopher (384–322BC) whose works, preserved and interpreted by Arabic philosophers, revolutionised Western philosophy when in the twelfth century they reached Paris from Moorish Spain
or fithele or gay sautrie:	fiddles and psalteries were popular instruments with students
philosophre:	(*i*) philosopher or natural scientist, hence (*ii*) alchemist, seeker after the philosopher's stone which converted base metal to gold. A pun
cofre:	chest
hente:	obtain. Students often had to beg for support
bisily:	earnestly
gan:	began
hem . . . scoleye:	those who gave him the means to study
cure:	care
o:	one
neede:	needful
forme:	due form
quyk:	pregnant
hy sentence:	elevated significance
Sownynge:	abounding (compare 275)

The Sergeant of the Law (lines 309–30)

Sergeants-at-Law (*servientes ad legem*) were the King's servants in legal matters, chosen from among the senior barristers. Those of them who were not judges could act as circuit judges, like Chaucer's Sergeant, but still pleaded in the courts and could grow rich on their fees. They were criticised for their purchases of land. One of these powerful men in 1386 was Thomas Pynchbec, and the possible pun in line 326 suggests that he may have been a source of this portrait.

NOTES AND GLOSSARY:

war:	cautious
Parvys:	Paradise, a name for the covered portico of a church, especially that of St Paul's, the cathedral of the City of London, the traditional meeting-place for lawyers and their clients
of:	in
He semed ... so wise:	He appeared to be so, for his words were so wise
Justice:	judge
assise:	assize or sitting of a court, held periodically in each county before judge and jury
patent:	patent, an open letter from the King
pleyn commissioun:	commission giving full powers
science:	knowledge
renoun:	reputation
robes:	given by clients in addition to their fees
many oon:	many a one
purchasour:	buyer-up (of land)
fee simple:	unrestricted ownership, a legal term
in effect:	in the end result
infect:	invalidated. (He made sure that his legal entitlement to any land he purchased was proof against legal challenge.)
nas:	was not
in termes:	in terms, precisely; even 'word for word'
caas:	cases. English common law is 'case-law', based on preceding decisions in similar cases
doomes:	decisions
William:	William the Conqueror, the Norman duke who conquered England in 1066 and established the administrative and legal system
were falle:	had occurred
endite:	write
make a thyng:	draw up a deed
pynche:	cavil
statut:	statute, Act of Parliament
coude:	knew
pleyn by rote:	completely by heart
He ... homely:	the dress in which he rode was plain
medlee:	of mixed weave

ceint:	girdle
barres smalle:	narrow stripes
telle I no lenger tale:	I say no more

The Franklin (lines 331–60)

A Franklin was a free man who held land direct from the Crown, without a Knight's obligation to military service. A country gentleman.

NOTES AND GLOSSARY:

dayesye:	daisy (literally 'day's eye'), the flower most often mentioned by Chaucer
complexioun:	refers not only to facial colour but to the temperament or combination of 'humours' which produced it. The four humours (hot, cold, moist and dry), themselves combinations of the four elements (earth, air, fire and water), produced four complexions (melancholy, choleric, phlegmatic and sanguine). In medieval medicine, a sanguine complexion (a combination of hot and moist humours) indicated self-indulgence
by the morwe:	in the morning
a sop in wyn:	a piece of cake dipped in wine
wone:	custom
Epicurus:	The austere Athenian philosopher (341–270BC), who held that pleasure, or the absence of pain, was the chief good. His 'Sons', the Epicureans, were later supposed to be gourmets or epicures
pleyn delit:	complete pleasure
verray felicitee parfit:	true and perfect happiness
Julian:	Julian the Hospitaller, a legendary saint famed for his hospitality
contree:	part of the world
after oon:	of one standard (namely the best)
bettre envyned:	with a better cellar
mete:	food
flessh:	meat
plentevous:	plentiful
snewed:	snowed
After:	according to
soper:	supper
partrich:	partridge
muwe:	cage
breem:	bream

luce:	pike
stewe:	fish-pond (*not* stew)
wo was:	unhappiness was the lot of
but if:	unless
geere:	utensils for the table
poynaunt:	piquant
table dormant:	a fixed table
al . . . day:	all day long
At sessions . . . lord and sire:	he presided over the sessions of the county court (see 314)
Knight of the shire:	Member of Parliament for the county
anlaas:	dagger
gipser:	purse
morne:	morning
shirreve:	sherriff, the King's steward (reeve) in a county (shire); the most important office after the Lord Lieutenant of a county
contour:	auditor of county finances
vavasour:	large landholder

The Five Guildsmen (lines 361–78)

A guild was originally the fraternity of a trade, but by the fourteenth century there were also religious and social guilds. As the five tradesmen each have a different craft, the guild whose livery they wear here must be religious. Guilds were the organisms of social life in medieval cities; their property was confiscated under Edward VI.

NOTES AND GLOSSARY:

Haberdasshere:	retailer of small articles of dress
Webbe:	weaver
Dyer:	dyer of cloth
Tapycer:	tapestry-maker
o lyveree:	the same livery or uniform
greet:	important
geere:	gear
apiked:	picked out, trimmed
chaped:	mounted. (Tradesmen and mechanics were forbidden by sumptuary law to have silver mountings)
wroght:	made
everydeel:	in every way
burgeys:	burgess, established citizen
yeldehalle:	guild hall, seat of city government
deys:	dais, platform

kan:	knows
shaply:	suited
alderman:	civic officer assisting the mayor
catel:	property
rente:	income
assente:	certify (to their wealth)
elles:	otherwise
to blame:	to be blamed
ycleped:	called
vigilies:	vigils, the eves of feast-days, when the guild would go to its chapel
roialliche ybore:	royally carried for you (by a servant)

The Cook (lines 379–87)

The cook retained by the guildsmen for the pilgrimage is a vulgar caterer rather than a chef, to judge by his repertoire, not to mention his tale and his drunken fall from his horse at the end of the pilgrimage.

NOTES AND GLOSSARY:

for the nones:	for the occasion
marybones:	marrow bones
poudre-marchant:	flavouring powder
tart:	tart, sharp-tasting
galingale:	sweet cyperus root, a spice like ginger
Wel . . . knowe:	he knew well how to recognise
London ale:	considered the best
koude . . . sethe:	knew how to roast and boil
mortreux:	a stew, the elements of which were prepared in a mortar
pye:	pie
thoughte me:	seemed to me
shyne:	shin
mormal:	a dried-up ulcer
For:	as for
blankmanger:	a mousse, of grated capon boiled in milk and sugar (*not* blancmange)
with:	equal to

The Shipman (lines 388–410)

The Shipman is the master of his barge, the Maudelayne. Dartmouth, two hundred miles from London, on the south coast of Devon, was then an important port. The Bordeaux trade was the heart of the wine business, in which Chaucer's family had engaged for generations. As a customs officer, he would have been well-informed about shipmen.

NOTES AND GLOSSARY:

woning . . . weste:	dwelling far to the west
woot:	know
rouncy:	a powerful horse; or, possibly, a nag
as he couthe:	as he knew how (that is, poorly)
laas:	lace, cord (like the lanyard of the Royal Navy)
felawe:	companion
ydrawe:	(*i*) carried as cargo; (*ii*) stolen secretly
Fro Burdeux-ward:	coming from Bordeaux (the wine port of Aquitaine, formerly an English possession)
chapman:	merchant
nyce:	delicate
keep:	heed
faught:	fought (with pirates)
hyer hand:	upper hand, victory
sent . . . home:	A euphemism for a common practice: he threw his prisoners into the sea
craft:	skill (*not* ship)
hym bisides:	which affected him
herberwe:	harbour
lodemenage:	pilotage (The 'lodestar' is the North Star, which 'leads' navigators.)
noon swich:	none like him
Hulle:	the port in the north of England
Cartage:	Cartagena, a port in Spain
Hardy:	tough
wys to undertake:	prudent in an undertaking
Gootland:	Gotland; the Baltic island with its port, Visby
Fynystere:	Finisterra, Spain (*not* Finisterre, Brittany)
cryke:	creek, harbour
Britaigne:	Brittany (*not* Britain)
Maudelayne:	A vessel of this name is recorded in Dartmouth in 1379 and in 1391, when its master was a Peter Risshenden. A barge was a trading vessel of between 100 and 200 tons

The Doctor of Physic (lines 411–44)

The Physician is, even more than most of the pilgrims, a master of his art, which then included astrology as well as other sciences which seem like witchcraft to modern Western medicine. His authorities are the ancient and the Arabic doctors. His professional skills are more impressive than his personal character.

NOTES AND GLOSSARY:

To speke of:	if we consider
astronomye:	we should call this astrology
kepte:	watched
In houres:	according to the hours (at which the various planetary influences affected the patient)
magyk natureel:	astrology (which dealt with the 'natural' heavenly bodies, not with spirits, like black magic)
Wel koude he . . . ascendent:	He knew well how to find the Ascendent in a favourable position (The Ascendent is the Zodiacal sign rising above the eastern horizon; whether or not it is 'fortunate' depends upon the conjunction of the planets, which the Doctor foresees.)
images:	talismans associated with Zodiacal signs
everich maladye:	every illness
Were it . . . drye:	See note to *complexioun* on page 24
praktisour:	practitioner
The cause . . . roote:	Once the cause was known and the source of his disease
Anon . . . boote:	He (the doctor) straightaway gave the sick man his remedy
drogges:	drugs
letuaries:	remedies
For . . . wynne:	For each of them made the other to gain
newe to bigynne:	newly begun
Esculapius:	the legendary father of medicine, Aesculapius, was a Greek god, supposed in the middle ages to be the author of several books. He begins a list of fifteen medical authorities, Greek, Arab and modern. Thus Dioscorides wrote in the first century AD, Rufus in the second, as did Galen, the greatest medical authority of antiquity. Hippocrates, the founder of Greek medical science, flourished in the fifth century BC; doctors still swear the Hippocratic oath of confidentiality. Haly may be the Persian Hali ibn el Abbas (died 994)
Serapion:	an Arab writer of the eleventh century
Razis . . . :	Rhazes (of Baghdad), Avicenna (of Bokhara) and Averroes (of Cordoba), famous Arabian philosophers of the eleventh and twelfth centuries
Damascien:	this may refer to the writings of two authors

Constantyn: a monk of Carthage who brought Arabian learning to Salerno in the eleventh century

Bernard ... Gilbertyn: a modern British trio: Bernard Gordon, a Scot, Professor of Medicine at Montpellier about 1300; John of Gaddesden of Merton College, Oxford, who died in 1361; Gilbertus Anglicus lived in the later thirteenth century

His studie ... Bible: Scepticism is still commonly alleged against doctors

sangwyn: red cloth

pers: a Persian blue-grey cloth

taffata: taffeta

sendal: a thin silk

esy of dispence: slow to spend money

that: what

pestilence: plague-time. The Black Death of 1349, which killed a third of the population of England, was the worst of four major outbreaks of bubonic plague in Chaucer's day

For: because

cordial: gold indeed formed part of prescriptions, but the next line is another comment on the doctor's avarice

The Wife of Bath (lines 445–76)

The Wife comes from the cloth-making neighbourhood of Bath, and is, like other pilgrims, skilful in her profession, which she was allowed to practise as the widow of a guildsman. However, the Wife (that is, woman) has also been a wife five times, and, as she explains at length in the Prologue to her tale, she is looking for her sixth husband, despite her age. This may be the reason she is so keen on pilgrimages.

NOTES AND GLOSSARY:

biside: nearby. The parish of St Michael's-juxta-Bathon was a centre of cloth-making. The weaving trade made the West Country rich in the middle ages

somdel deef: somewhat deaf—as the result of a blow on the ear from her fifth husband, as recounted in the Wife's Prologue

scathe: a pity

haunt: skill

passed: surpassed

Gaunt: Ghent; like Ypres, a centre of Flemish weaving. Edward III attracted many Flemish weavers to settle in England, and improved the weaving of English wool

In al the parisshe . . . noon: Not a woman in the whole parish

offrynge: Offertory, the part of the Mass when the people offer gifts. Today ushers collect money, but in medieval churches the people went up to the altar in order of social precedence (see 377) with gifts of their own manufacture

bifore: in front of

ther dide: any woman were to do so

wrooth: angry

out of alle charitee: beyond thought of being charitable (Ironic, because the Offertory was a time for being generous)

coverchiefs: head-coverings

fine . . . of ground: finely woven

weyeden ten pound: weighed ten pounds

hosen: stockings (The Wife's Sunday offering was a walking advertisement for her wares, and for herself.)

streite: tightly

moyste: soft

fair: pleasing

hewe: hue

lyve: life

at chirche dore: in front of the church door (where all marriages took place)

Withouten: not counting

oother compaignye: a hint at her promiscuity

nedeth nat: it is not necessary

as nowthe: for the present, just now

Jerusalem: pronounced 'Jersalem'. Pilgrimages to the Holy Land were not uncommon, although in going thrice (*thries*) the Wife is excessive

straunge strem: foreign river

Rome: where, for example, Saints Peter and Paul were martyred

Boloigne: Boulogne-sur-Mer, where an image of the Virgin Mary is venerated

Galice at Seint Jame: the very popular shrine of St James the Greater, at Compostella, Galicia, north-west Spain

Coloigne: the shrine of the Three Kings of the East (the Magi of the Epiphany), who ended their travels at Cologne in Germany

She koude ... weye: She knew a lot about wandering off the road. (The Wife dallied off the 'straight and narrow way' of Matthew 7:14)

Gat-tothed: gate-toothed; with teeth widely spaced. The Wife in line 603 of her Prologue associates this with Venus

amblere: an ambling horse

esily: in a relaxed way

sat: she rides astride in the Ellesmere MS illustration. (The fashion of riding side-saddle was introduced into England by Anne of Bohemia, Richard II's first wife.)

bokeler or a targe: buckler or a shield

foot-mantel: a riding-skirt, or outer skirt

large: ample (the skirt, not the hips)

spores: spurs

felaweship: company

carpe: talk

the olde daunce: a proverbial phrase, like 'all the ins and outs'

The Parson (lines 477–528)

The Parson is the ideal parish priest, free from the faults both of the regular clergy already described and of some parish priests. He cares for his flock rather than himself, and his treasure is in heaven. He is described in terms of his virtues rather than his tastes or appearance.

NOTES AND GLOSSARY:

toun: village

parisshens: parishioners, inhabitants of his parish

wonder: wonderfully

ypreved ... sithes: often proven

Ful looth ... tithes: He was very reluctant to excommunicate for his tithes. Laymen were obliged to give one-tenth of their income or produce to support their priest. Non-payment could mean exclusion from the sacrament of communion

But ... out of doute: But, beyond doubt, he would rather give

aboute: in the parish

offryng: The money given at the Offertory (see 450) at Easter supports the priest

substaunce: property

koude: knew how to (see *Truth*, p.49)

fer asonder: far apart

meschief: misfortune

muche and lite:	great and small
upon . . . a staf:	According to the example of early Christian pastors
gospel:	Matthew 5:19
figure:	analogy
That . . . do:	A traditional image
lewed:	unlearned
rust:	rust, tarnish
keep:	heed
shiten:	covered in excrement
Wel oghte . . . yive:	It well becomes a priest to set an example
sette . . . hire:	did not rent out his living. Absentee parsons appointed vicars and curates
And leet . . . myre:	Nor left his sheep encumbered in the bog (of sin)
To seken . . . soules:	To get himself a chantry for souls. A chantry was a provision for a priest to say (or chant) a daily mass for the repose of the soul of a deceased person—an easier life than that of a country parish
Or . . . withholde:	Or to be retained by a guild (as chaplain)
Kepte . . . folde:	kept watch over his sheepfold
myscarie:	come to destruction
mercenarie:	hireling. 512–4 are based on John's Gospel 10:12. The 'wolf' represents the Devil
despitous:	contemptuous
daungerous ne digne:	arrogant nor haughty
discreet:	courteous
fairnesse:	attraction
his bisynesse:	what he worked for
But:	unless
What so:	whatever
lough estat:	low position
snybben:	rebuke
for the nonys:	for that reason
trowe:	believe
nowher noon ys:	is none anywhere
He . . . reverence:	He expected no reverence
spiced:	over-scrupulous
loore:	teaching
apostles twelve:	That is, their example
He taughte . . . hymselve:	The parson practised what he preached

The Ploughman (lines 529–41)

The Ploughman is brother to the Parson, and is equally ideal. With the Knight, these two brothers express English medieval social ideals. He is a hard worker who loves God and his neighbour, serves others and pays his tithes. This last indicates that, though a peasant, the Ploughman is a small tenant farmer, and a free man rather than a serf.

NOTES AND GLOSSARY:

was:	'he' is understood
y-lad . . . fother:	pulled many a cart-load of dung
A trewe . . . was he:	He was a good hard worker. (Compare the modern English 'a good man and true'.)
charitee:	the supreme theological virtue, defined in the next lines in the words of Christ's supreme commandment
hoole:	whole
though . . . smerte:	whether it was pleasant or painful to him
and . . . delve:	and also dig ditches and make hedges
poure wight:	poor creature
hire:	payment
myghte:	power
tythes:	tenth part of a man's produce, due to the Church
propre swynk:	own labour (that is, the corn from the fields he ploughed)
catel:	property, possessions (*not* cows)
mere:	mare (regarded as an inferior mount)
namo:	no more

The Miller (lines 545–66)

The Miller leads the rascally final group of pilgrims. A mill had the monopoly of grinding all the corn on each manor, and could charge a high price. This miller was strong and quarrelsome, which made it easier for him to abuse his monopoly.

NOTES AND GLOSSARY:

stout:	sturdy
carl:	churl, fellow
for the nones:	indeed
proved:	was shown
over al:	everywhere
ther he cam:	where he went
ram:	the prize in a wrestling match
knarre:	knot
Ther . . . harre:	there was no door that he could not heave off its hinge
at a renning:	with a single charge

berd:	beard
reed:	red
Upon . . . right:	right on the top of
werte:	wart
tofte of herys:	tuft of hairs
brustles:	bristles
erys:	ears
nosethirles:	nostrils
bar:	carried
forneys:	furnace
janglere . . . goliardeys: gossip and a ribald talker	
that:	his talk
harlotries:	dirty jokes
Wel koude . . . thries: he knew well how to steal corn and charge three times over	
thombe of golde:	The proverb 'Every honest miller has a thumb of gold' means that there are no honest millers and few poor ones. The miller's thumb tested the corn and weighed out the flour
pardee:	by God
sowne:	sound
therwithal he broughte: with it he accompanied	

The Manciple (lines 567–86)

A manciple was a servant of a college or inn of court, who purchased the provisions, under the direction of the cook and the steward.

NOTES AND GLOSSARY:

gentil:	pleasant
temple:	the Middle and the Inner Temple are two of the lawyers' Inns of Court in London
Of which achatours: from whom purchasers (caterers)	
vitaille:	victuals
taille:	tally, credit
algate:	always
wayted:	paid attention
achaat:	buying
ay biforn:	always in front
staat:	state, condition
grace:	grace, favour
lewed:	uneducated (*not* lewd)
wit:	intelligence
pace:	surpass

heepe:	heap
maistres:	masters, lawyers who have qualified by being called to the bar
mo than thries:	more than thrice
of:	in
curious:	intimately interested
duszeyne:	dozen
stywardes:	stewards
hym:	the lord
lyve by:	sustain himself upon
propre good:	own property
dettelees:	without indebtedness
but . . . wood:	unless he were mad
scarsely:	economically
hym list desire:	it might please him to desire
And . . . shire:	And capable to help [administer] a whole county
caas:	situation
falle:	come about
sette . . . cappe:	set the caps of them all (made them look silly)

The Reeve (lines 587–622)

A reeve was the bailiff or factor for an estate—today's estate-manager. Like the Manciple and others among the middle-class pilgrims, he makes dishonest profits. He was trained as a carpenter in youth and is later angered by the Miller's Tale against a carpenter; the Miller rides first, the Reeve last.

NOTES AND GLOSSARY:

sclendre colerik:	thin, angry (see note on p.24)
ny:	nigh, near, close
His heer . . . yshorn:	his hair was cut round his head at the height of his ears
top was dokked:	top was cut short
biforn:	in front. Priests wore a tonsure, but also kept their hair short in front
lene:	lean
staf:	staff, stick
ysene:	to be seen
gerner:	granary
bynne:	chest
auditour:	auditor, accountant
on him wynne:	get the better of him
wiste:	knew

droghte . . . reyn:	drought and rain
yeldynge:	yield
neet:	cattle
swyn, his hors:	swine [plural] and horses
stoor:	livestock
pultrye:	poultry
governyng:	control
by his covenant:	according to his agreement (legal deed of service)
yaf the rekenynge:	gave the reckoning
syn that:	since
brynge . . . arrerage:	cause him to be behind (in collecting money due to him)
baillif:	bailiff, steward
hierde:	shepherd
hyne:	hind, servant
That . . . covyne:	that the reeve did not know about his deceit and his fraudulent agreement
adrad:	in dread, terrified
wonyng:	dwelling
purchase:	buy (land) (See 320)
astored pryvely:	provisioned secretly
To yeve . . . good:	to give and lend him from out of his (the lord's) own goods
cote and hood:	the coat and hood were a servant's perquisite; thanks are due only to an equal or superior
myster:	trade, occupation (French *métier*)
stot:	horse, cob
pomely:	dapple
highte:	was called
surcote of pers:	blue overcoat
Northfolk:	Norfolk, an East Anglian county
toun:	village
clepen Baldeswelle:	call Bawdswell
tukked:	tucked. His robe was hitched up round him into his girdle, as a friar's is
hyndreste of oure route:	hindmost of our crowd

The Summoner (lines 623–68)

A summoner summonsed accused persons to the Bishop's Court. Ecclesiastical law operated alongside civil law and had jurisdiction over lay people as well as clerics. The church courts dealt with a range of offences, such as sexual immorality, witchcraft and withholding of tithes. The Bishop's Archdeacon, who presided, imposed fines backed by the threat of excommunication; excommunication could lead to imprisonment by the civil authorities. Consequently the summoner, as officer of the court, could easily extort money from the weak.

NOTES AND GLOSSARY:

fyr-reed . . . face:	the face of a cherub, as red as fire. Although cherubs, or cherubim, were supposed to have red faces, it is implied that the Summoner did not look like an angelic messenger
sawcefleem:	pimpled (from 'salt phlegm')
eyen narwe:	narrow eyes
sparwe:	the sparrow was traditionally considered to be very lecherous
scaled:	scaly, scabby
piled:	scanty
lytarge:	white lead
boras:	borax
ceruce:	white lead
tartre:	tartar
noon:	not any kind
byte:	bite, scour
whelkes:	pimples
knobbes:	lumps
crie:	shout
wood:	mad
decree:	decree (of canon law)
Watte:	Wat (short for 'Walter')
grope:	examine minutely, probe
Ay . . . crie:	he would always cry: 'Questio quid juris'. (A Latin legal tag meaning 'I ask which law applies to this case'.)
gentil harlot:	easy-going rascal. ('Harlot' was applied exclusively to women only in the next century.)
suffer:	allow
for:	in return for
have:	keep, enjoy
his:	the fellow's (not the Summoner's)
atte fulle:	at the end (of the year)
a fynch . . . pulle:	pluck the feathers of a finch (that is, a fool)
owher:	anywhere
a good felawe:	a good companion (that is, a rogue)
curs:	curse, excommunication
But if:	unless
in his purs:	By a fine

helle: an excommunicated person might go to hell for ever. The Summoner seems to consider a fine to be a worse punishment

woot ... dede: know that in reality he was lying

Of cursyng ... drede: Every guilty man ought to be afraid of excommunication

For curs ... savith: For excommunication will kill, just as absolution will save

And ... Significavit: And he [the guilty man] should also beware of a *Significavit*. (This was the opening Latin word of a writ issued by the Archdeacon to the civil authorities certifying that an excommunicated man had remained obstinate after forty days; the penalty was imprisonment.)

daunger: jurisdiction, control

at ... gise: to do with as he liked

girles: the young of both sexes

diocise: diocese (the area over which a bishop has responsibility)

hir conseil: their secrets

al hir reed: their only counsellor

gerland: garland (of leaves and flowers)

greet: large

ale-stake: taverns used to advertise themselves by hanging a bush or garland from a pole outside

bokeleer: buckler, shield

cake: loaf (held in his lap)

The Pardoner (lines 669–714)

A pardoner sold pardons or indulgences. These were remissions of penances imposed in the confessional, or of punishment in Purgatory. (They were not pardons for sins, for such pardon is available only to the repentant sinner.) Pardons were certificates of remission of penance, and were introduced in return for gifts to an ecclesiastical charity. The system got out of control and was abused, for example by unlicensed pardoners who sold false relics. The sale of indulgences was one of the abuses that provoked the Reformers. The Pardoner is the last of the pilgrims, and the most corrupt.

NOTES AND GLOSSARY:

Rouncivale: The hospital of St Mary, Rounceval, near Charing Cross, London. (Rounceval belonged to the Prior of Rouncevall in Navarre.)

compeer:	fellow, crony
court of Rome:	The Pardoner claims to come from the Roman Curia, the source of authorised indulgences
"Come . . . to me":	A popular song. Note rhyme of 'Rome' and 'to me'
bar . . . burdoun:	accompanied him in a strong bass. (Possibly a homosexual relationship is suggested.)
trompe:	trumpet
wex:	wax
But . . . flex:	but it hung straight, as does a hank of flax
By ounces . . . hadde:	the few locks that he had hung separately
And . . . overspradde:	and he spread them over his shoulders
But . . . oon:	but the hair lay thin in single shreds
But . . . noon:	but he wore no hood, out of jollity
Hym thoughte:	it seemed to him, he fancied
of the newe jet:	in the latest fashion
Dischevelee, save:	dishevelled, except for
vernycle:	Veronica. (After St Veronica, who offered her veil to Christ on the way to Calvary so that he could wipe his face. The veil, with the impression of Christ's face, was kept at St Peter's in Rome. Pilgrims to Rome often wore copies of it.)
sowed:	sewed
Bretful:	full to the brim
pardon:	pardons
hoot:	Like cakes freshly made (part of the Pardoner's sales-talk)
smal . . . goot:	thin as a goat has; that is, unbroken
late:	recently
trow:	believe
gelding:	a castrated horse
mare:	female horse. The Pardoner is effeminate
fro . . . Ware:	from Berwick-on-Tweed to Ware, Hertfordshire. (That is, from the north of England to the south, as these towns are at each end of the Great North Road from London to Scotland.)
male:	mail bag
pilwe-beer:	pillowcase
Oure Lady veyl:	the veil of Our Lady (as Catholics call Mary)
gobet:	gobbet, piece
seyl:	sail
wente:	walked
see:	sea
hente:	took up, saved (see Mark 15:7–11)
croys of latoun:	crucifix of brass

relikes:	relics. A Catholic altar incorporates a physical relic of a martyr. The cult of relics was widespread as an incentive to faith and piety
A povre . . . lond:	A poor parson living in his country parish
Upon . . . moneye:	In one day he got for himself more money
tweye:	two
feyned:	feigned
japes:	tricks
apes:	gulls, fools
trewely to tellen:	to tell truly
ecclesiaste:	the Pardoner was probably not a cleric
lessoun:	lesson (a Bible reading)
storie:	such as a Saint's Life, or the Pardoner's own moral tale
alderbest:	best of all
offertorie:	anthem sung at the offertory (see 450)
wiste:	knew
preche:	preach
affile:	smooth
murierly:	more merrily

Recapitulation (lines 715–24)

NOTES AND GLOSSARY:

clause:	short sentence
staat:	condition
Belle:	the Bell, another hostelry
to yow . . . telle:	to tell you
How . . . nyght:	what we did with ourselves that same night
alyght:	alighted, settled
wol:	will
viage:	journey

Apology (lines 725–46)

NOTES AND GLOSSARY:

narette:	do not impute
vileynye:	ill-breeding, grossness
cheere:	demeanour
Ne . . . properly:	not even if I speak their words with accuracy in each case
also:	as
He moot . . . kan:	he should repeat, as closely as he can
Everich . . . charge:	every word, if it is entrusted to him (to do so)

Al . . . large:	Although he [the man] speak never so rudely and freely
untrewe:	falsely
feyne thyng:	feign things
spare:	relent
he:	the man of line 731
moot as well:	must equally
Crist . . . writ:	Christ himself spoke very broadly in the Scriptures
woot:	know
Plato:	An allusion to the Greek philosopher's *Timaeus* (29B), known to Chaucer through Boethius, whom he had translated
rede:	read. Greek was extinct in England at this time
moote be cosyn:	must be cousin
Al:	although, if
degree:	social rank
My wit is short:	I am not very clever

The tale-telling game: the Host's proposal (lines 747–809)

NOTES AND GLOSSARY:

Greet . . . everichon:	our host entertained us all very cheerfully
soper:	supper (a communal meal)
leste:	it pleased
semely:	fit, suitable
Hooste:	Host, innkeeper. Although not a pilgrim, the Host is, from the point of view of the narrative, as important as any of them, since he organises the tale-telling game. The Host's name is revealed much later when the Cook calls him Harry Bailly. An innkeeper of this name is mentioned in the records for Southwark at this period, so the character of the Host must bear some relationship to a real-life contemporary of Chaucer—though the relationship may very well be quite as unstraightforward as that between Chaucer the pilgrim and Chaucer the man
withalle:	moreover, too
For . . . halle:	[fit] to have been a marshal [master of ceremonies] in a hall
Chepe:	Cheapside, the marketplace of the City of London. Southwark was a much less respectable place than the City, so this line is a compliment to the Host's citizenship

ytaught:	trained in his trade
And . . . naught:	he was in no way lacking in manhood
pleyen:	to play, jest
maad our rekenynges:	paid our bills
lordynges:	my masters (used when addressing a company, like 'Ladies and Gentlemen')
Ye . . . hertely:	you are indeed heartily welcome to my house
ne saugh:	have not seen
ones:	once
herberwe:	harbour, inn
Fayn . . . how:	I would dearly like to entertain you, if I knew how
bythoght:	struck by a thought
God yow speede:	may God bring you success
The blisful . . . meede!:	may the blessed martyr bring you your reward
wel I woot:	as I well know
by the weye:	along the road
Ye . . . pleye:	you intend to tell stories and amuse yourselves
confort:	comfort
maken you disport:	devise entertainment for you
erst:	first
yow liketh:	it pleases you
stonden at:	stand by, accept
werken:	do
Now . . . deed:	now by my father's soul, who is dead
But . . . heed!:	if you are not merry, strike off my head
Hold . . . hondes:	in sign of agreement
Oure . . . seche:	it did not take long to discover our opinion
Us . . . wys:	we did not think it was worth while to deliberate seriously
avys:	consideration
verdit . . . leste:	verdict, as he pleased
quod:	said
herkneth . . . beste:	listen carefully
But . . . desdeyn:	but do not treat it with disdain, I beg you
pleyn:	plain
to . . . weye:	so to shorten our journey
tweye:	two
To . . . so:	I mean, on the way to Canterbury
And . . . two:	And he shall tell another two on the way home
Of . . . bifalle:	of adventures that have happened in the past
which:	the one
bereth him:	manages
in . . . caas:	on this occasion
sentence:	meaning, significance

solaas:	solace, comfort
oure aller cost:	the expense of the rest of us
agayn:	back
Right . . . cost:	at my own expense
gyde:	guide
And . . . withseye:	whoever shall dispute my judgement
paye al:	pay for all
vouchesauf:	vouchsafe
anon . . . mo:	immediately, without further discussion
erly . . . therefore:	get ready for the journey early

The tale-telling game: the pilgrims' acceptance (lines 810–21)

NOTES AND GLOSSARY:

and . . . swore:	and we swore our oaths
governour:	president
juge and reportour:	judge and reporter
And . . . pris:	And arrange a supper at a set price
And . . . devys:	And we will be ruled as he shall devise
In . . . assent:	In great things and small; and so, unanimously
fet anon:	fetched immediately
We . . . echon:	We drank, and went to bed each of us

The tale-telling game: the setting-forth (lines 822–41)

NOTES AND GLOSSARY:

Amorwe:	in the morning
cok:	cock, the male bird who leads the hens out
riden . . . paas:	rode, at little more than a walking pace
wateryng . . . Thomas:	A brook near the second milestone on the Canterbury road, where pilgrims watered their horses
bigan . . . arest:	pulled his horse up
Ye . . . recorde:	You know your promise, and I remind you of it
If . . . accorde:	If evening-song and morning-song agree. (That is, if the pilgrims have not changed their tune.)
mote:	may. 'As truly as I wish to go on drinking . . .'
draweth:	the first of four polite plural imperatives, addressed to the more gentle pilgrims
cut:	cut, draw lots. (Different lengths, perhaps of straw, are to be drawn from the Host's hand to decide who tells the first tale. The Host doubtless arranges that the Knight should draw the short straw.)
accord:	decision
lat . . . shamefastnesse:	leave aside your modesty

'Ne . . . man!':   'Forget your philosophy; put out your hand and take your straw, everyone.'

The tale-telling game: the cut (lines 842–58)

NOTES AND GLOSSARY:

Were . . . cas:	Either by luck, or fate, or chance
sothe:	sooth, truth
fil:	fell
And . . . resoun:	And tell his tale he must, as was reasonable
composicioun:	agreement
As . . . mo?:	As you have heard; what more needs to be said?
As he that:	as a man who
by . . . assent:	(given) by his free consent
a:	by
herkneth:	listen

Part 3

Commentary

THE NATURE of *The Canterbury Tales* is various, since it consists of a miscellany of tales such as might be told by a mixed group of pilgrims on the road to Canterbury. The work is united by the framework of the tale-telling competition, and though this competition is not completed, the design of the work is clear, and so is the significance of its final pattern.

The *General Prologue* is an expository introduction and overture to the *Tales*, introducing both the tellers and the themes of the pilgrimage. Because it is itself so entertaining, varied and self-contained, and because it has a vivid freshness like that of medieval manuscript illuminations and stained glass windows, it is often read on its own. Thus detached, it can be taken as Chaucer's picture of the society of his time, especially as the gallery of portraits of the pilgrims is a fairly representative cross-section of those who were free to go on a pilgrimage. Also, it is written in a vivid and realistic style, so that we can imagine that Chaucer did meet actual people resembling his fellow-pilgrims. Chaucer's story-telling art allows us to combine with the interest of understanding something of medieval society the pleasure of becoming involved with a 'real' set of people.

The *Prologue* was, however, intended as a prologue, to be imagined as spoken by Chaucer himself (as no doubt it was at its first performance to the court of Richard II). It would thus have been read to an audience who knew him well and would have enjoyed the idea of his accidentally falling in with a ready-made group of pilgrims, and of their fictional adventures. They would have certainly been amused at the figure Chaucer cuts later in the *Tales*. The Host addresses him as a fat little man, too shy to tell a story. When pressed, the pilgrim Chaucer begins on a feeble romance, a parody of bad popular romances: it rhymes so wretchedly that the Host cannot endure it and rudely prevents Chaucer from continuing. Like the original audience, we too know that this supposedly autobiographical story is not entirely true: if Chaucer did go on such a pilgrimage, it is not likely that its members spoke in verse, nor that their tales would have been audible from horseback. The appearance of verisimilitude is brilliant and intense, but it is a deliberate illusion, which Chaucer dispenses with in many of the tales themselves, though he returns to the appearance of naturalism between them.

Realism

Like all great artists, Chaucer is a realist. But we should recall that it would not have occurred to him to write a naturalistic novel or a piece of social history. The portraits of the pilgrims are introduced partly, and perhaps chiefly, because the tales which are to follow must have tellers to tell them. On examination, each of the portraits can be seen to be formal and self-contained, as they are not in naturalistic novels. Also, improbably, the portraits represent persons all of entirely different professions (with the exception of five identical Guildsmen). This is also non-naturalistic, but it lends some support to the idea that Chaucer had some historical intention of creating a representative cross-section of society, or rather of the middle class, since both top and bottom of society are excluded. Pilgrimages would not include serfs or poor peasants, who were not free to travel; a nobleman would travel with his private retinue; and women would normally have to stay at home, unless they were independent, like the Prioress or the Wife of Bath—two women among twenty men.

Of course, Chaucer could not be aware that readers five centuries later would think of him and his pilgrims as typically medieval, and his intentions differed from those of, say, George Eliot, who certainly meant the characters of her novel *Middlemarch* (published in 1872) to represent the life of a country town in the English midlands of the early nineteenth century. So long as we bear this in mind, there is no harm in seeing the pilgrims as representative English men and women of the later middle ages. Indeed it is inevitable that we should do so, for they are conceived as typical human beings, and thus have a social and economic as well as a spiritual and moral dimension. Many of them are types who would have been familiar to lettered and even unlettered people in the audience: the hunting monk, the venal friar, the dedicated knight, the gay young squire, the ladylike prioress, the piratical ship-man. All these were figures known to popular as well as literary tradition, either as caricatures or as ideals. Similar caricatures of the clergy are to be found, for example, in the contemporary poem *Piers Plowman*, as is the figure of an idealised ploughman.

The portraits should not be allowed to dominate the *Prologue* to the exclusion of what precedes and follows them. Unlike the series of full-length portraits, which, however lively, remains somewhat static, the introduction to the portraits is narrative and dramatic, and its sequel is much more so: the pilgrims step out of their portraits and talk, quarrel and drink; one of them even falls off his horse. The introduction, and the proposal and acceptance of the tale-telling game, present us with two further pilgrims, who are dramatised rather than described: the pilgrim Chaucer, our guide, and the Host, our master of ceremonies.

The portraits belong to the context of the *Prologue* and they should be seen in that context, as the *Prologue* only comes into its own when the whole of *The Canterbury Tales* is read. The portraits are part of a developing fictional action, as well as illustrating the most brilliant page in English medieval social history. To use a theatrical analogy, it is rather as if *The Canterbury Tales* opened with the cast assembled on the stage at the beginning instead of at the end of a play. A true historical sense involves us in seeing these characters as living: when we see the Merchant, we see the eternal pompous businessman, and not just a typical representative of an emerging class in the City of London in the late fourteenth century. Later on he turns out to be unhappily married, and becomes even more of a human being than the representative of a class.

Here is a last point about Chaucer's illusion of verisimilitude: he apologises for the random informality of the order in which he presents the pilgrims:

> Also I prey yow to foryeve it me,
> Al have I nat set folk in hir degree.
>
> (743–4)

But this modesty is partly a joke, for he has in fact set folk in their degree, according to a hierarchy which is both social and moral: the Knight is at the top and the Pardoner is at the bottom. The military Estate is followed by the clerical Estate; the clerics by the laity; the upper-middle class by the lower-middle class; with the rascals at the end. Further, within this apparently casual order of descending importance and merit, there is another kind of order created by dramatic contrasts in juxtaposition: the Knight fights for his Lord, the Squire for his Lady; the Merchant's talk is full of his prospering business, the Clerk's of moral virtue; the Clerk's cope is threadbare, the Friar's is new. On inspection, the *General Prologue* is found to have a rich unobtrusive moral pattern. It is not only a historically representative cross-section of social types, nor an impression of some striking individuals. Like Shakespeare and the great novelists, Chaucer in *The Canterbury Tales* gives us a representation of the human comedy, not of his day only but of all time. As the neo-classical poet and critic John Dryden (1631–1700) said:

> 'Tis sufficient to say according to the proverb, that here is God's plenty. We have our forefathers and great-grand-dames all before us, as they were in Chaucer's days; their general characters are still remaining in mankind, and even in England, though they are called by other names . . . For mankind is ever the same, and nothing lost out of Nature, though everything is altered.

The first of the Romantic poets, William Blake (1757–1827), agreed:

> Of Chaucer's characters, as described in *The Canterbury Tales*, some of the names or titles are altered by time, but the characters themselves remain unaltered, and consequently they are the phisiognomies or lineaments of universal life, beyond which Nature never steps.

Christian comedy

Chaucer is a comic writer with a rich and varied sense of humanity, yet *The Canterbury Tales* is more than a *human* comedy: it is God's plenty. Comedy in the medieval sense of the word has perhaps some relevance to it. At the end of his great tragedy, *Troilus and Criseyde* (which he calls 'litel myn tragedye'), Chaucer prays that God will send him the ability to try his hand in 'some comedye'. Dante (1265–1321) had entitled his pilgrimage through Hell and Purgatory to Heaven the *Commedia*, not because it was humorous but because it ends in a happier state than it began. Chaucer's *Tales* are a large and various work, where the part obscures the whole, where we shift between the tellers and their tales, and where the design is not fully completed. However, the pilgrimage is more than a device. The Parson, a wholly ideal character, tells the last tale, late in the evening as the shadows are lengthening. It is an uncompromising sermon on the necessity for repentance, and comes as a shock. We realise that, from the Knight's 'noble storie' onwards, the pleasant pilgrimage has progressively declined into a comic, quarrelsome, blasphemous and sometimes brutal chaos, culminating in the Cook's drunken fall from his horse into the slough. The nearer the pilgrims get to Canterbury, the more their fallibility appears. The Parson asks Jesus for his grace:

> 'To shewe yow the wey, in this viage,
> Of thilke parfit glorious pilgrymage,
> That highte Jerusalem celestial.'
> (X, 49–51)

Here the Parson is speaking allegorically: the way to the heavenly Jerusalem is by the path of repentance—a straight and narrow way very unlike the broad and easy human road to Canterbury. There are many glimpses, hints and reminders of this higher road among the more sinful as well as the more pious tales. Nevertheless, despite the comic delight in and understanding of human self-delusion, and despite all its abounding charity towards the sinner, Chaucer's human world is profoundly and instinctively organised by the Christian understanding of life which appears so starkly in the *Parson's Tale*.

The *General Prologue* is so sunny, sane, earthly and human that it may be necessary to emphasise that although Chaucer may be the first humanist in English literature and the first realist in portraying personal and social relations, he remains also a medieval Christian in his sense of man's impermanence and of the supreme importance of the divine perspective. This perspective appears only occasionally and obliquely in the *Prologue*, which is largely static, with little dramatic interaction between the characters, but the claims of Christ colour the portraits of the knight, parson and ploughman. This perennial Christian philosophy is expressed most economically and fully outside the *Tales*, in Chaucer's most popular poem in manuscripts, *Truth*, or the *Balade de Bon Conseyl*.

> Flee fro the prees, and dwelle with sothfastnesse,
> Suffyce unto thy good, though it be smal;
> For hord hath hate, and climbing tikelnesse,
> Prees hath envye, and wele blent overal;
> Savour no more than thee bihove shal;
> Reule wel thyself, that other folk canst rede;
> And trouthe thee shal delivere, it is no drede.

> Tempest thee noght al croked to redresse,
> In trust of hir that turneth as a bal:
> Gret reste stant in litel besinesse;
> Be war also to sporne ayeyns an al;
> Stryve not, as doth the crokke with the wal.
> Daunte thyself, that dauntest otheres dede;
> And trouthe thee shal delivere, it is no drede.

> That thee is sent, receyve in buxumnesse;
> The wrastling for this world axeth a fal.
> Her is non hoom, her nis but wildernesse:
> Forth, pilgrim, forth! Forth, beste, out of thy stal!
> Know thy contree, look up, thank God of al;
> Hold the heye wey, and lat thy gost thee lede;
> And trouthe thee shal delivere, it is no drede.

This can be literally rendered:

Leave the throng of Court and make your home with Truth; content yourself with what you have, though it be slender. For hoarding is attended by hatred and worldly preferment by precariousness; the Court is full of envy, and success quite blinds its possessor; relish no more than what shall become you; govern yourself well, you who may counsel others; and Truth shall most certainly deliver you.

Do not torment yourself to reform all that is amiss, putting your trust in her who turns like a ball: great peace is to be found in little business; beware also of kicking against the pricks; do not strive as does the pot against the wall. Tame yourself, you who tame the actions of others; and Truth shall most certainly deliver you.

Accept with a good will what is sent you; wrestling for this world asks for a fall. There is no home here; here is nothing but a wilderness: out, pilgrim, out! Out, beast, out of thy stall! Acknowledge your native land—look up, thank God for everything: stick to the high road and let your spirit lead you; and Truth shall most certainly deliver you.

This advice is interesting, coming as it does from a man who seems quite at home in this world. It may be that Chaucer himself had discovered that 'The wrastling for this world axeth a fal'. But the philosophy is traditional—it has been described as a resumé of the *Consolation of Philosophy* of Boethius (AD *c*.480—524), a work which Chaucer translated, and one of the most popular and influential books of the middle ages. The *Consolation* is itself a resumé of Stoic and Platonic thinking on the Contempt of the World, as it was called in Christian tradition. Stoicism was a widespread classical philosophical and ethical system of thought centred on obedience to natural law. Plato (*c*.429–347 BC) taught that the world of physical appearances and events is unreal. Chaucer's Bon Conseyl, or Good Advice, is to scorn the rewards of this world in order to earn those of the next world, which is the homeland of the soul: 'Know thy contree'. The truth which shall set free the friend to whom the poem is written is the truth of St John's Gospel 8:32: 'Ye shall know the truth, and the truth shall make you free'. The philosophy of *Truth* is a synthesis of classical and Christian moral thought, in which biblical allusions mingle with classical maxims in a proverbial style which may surprise those who think of the middle ages as unfamiliar with classical tradition. The Sermon on the Mount of line 2 and the conversion of Saul (line 11) combine quite happily with Fortune (line 9), a classical goddess unknown to the Bible. The God who is to be thanked (line 19) is the God of Christian revelation, but the sentiments of the first two stanzas of the poem would be perfectly intelligible to an educated Roman pagan. The fundamental image of the poem is of life as a pilgrimage—a medieval image but not necessarily an ascetic one, as can be seen in the homely and humorous image of the pilgrim as a beast (line 18) to be led by its *gost*, as a cow is by the cowherd.

Truth is a valuable miniature introduction to the *General Prologue*, not only because it is a summary of the moral commonplaces of the age, but more specifically. The famous first paragraph of the *Prologue* is full of classical mythology and the Arabic astronomy of the Zodiac, and also of the natural history of a scientific sort, which places Nature (line 11) in an apparently sovereign position. Yet the paragraph ends with the simple piety of the English pilgrimage to Canterbury. It would be equally mistaken to ignore either the naturalism of the introduction or the supernaturalism of the conclusion. The two are blended in the rich synthesis of *Truth*, and in the same blend of an elevated and a homely style. Medieval Christianity was not the religion only of monks and ascetics: the whole of what we now think of as secular society was included in and dignified by the Incarnation, as was the natural world of bird and 'holt and heeth'. The spring which keeps the birds awake all night also moves folks to go on pilgrimage to thank the saint who has interceded for them in the winter when they were sick. It is natural for the poet thus to celebrate the physical world which, as he reminds us, we must ultimately leave behind.

Variety and unity

It is the achievement of *The Canterbury Tales* to combine in a simple narrative many varied and dramatic subjects of human interest, from the loftiest to the lowest. The unifying factors in this very diverse mass of material are several, and might be listed as follows:

(1) The narrative framework of the pilgrimage and tale-telling.

(2) The dramatic interplay between the characters of the pilgrims, either because their values differ (thus, the *Miller's Tale* mocks the idealism of the *Knight's Tale*) or because they are professional rivals (like the Friar and the Summoner, rival parasites upon the laity). The pilgrims argue with or tell tales against each other.

(3) The intellectual debate between the tales, for example on the subject of authority in marriage, the theme of the *Wife's Tale* and the *Clerk's Tale*.

(4) The role of the Host as master of ceremonies.

(5) The personality of the narrator, Chaucer the poet and pilgrim— not easily distinguished from his style.

(6) The complex of values indicated in the foregoing paragraphs—a medieval Christian humanism.

The second and third of these factors are not present to any extent in the *General Prologue*, and the first is only given an introductory sketch, as is the fourth. The fifth and sixth may be examined in a discussion of the strategy of the *General Prologue*, which divides into three parts: the pilgrimage, the pilgrims, and the tale-telling game. The middle part, the gallery of portraits of the pilgrims, is the largest and most significant, but the way we approach it is considerably affected by the more dramatic and narrative sections which frame it.

Chaucer the pilgrim

After the description of spring, already discussed, we hear (lines 30-2)
how Chaucer made himself one of the pilgrims:

> And shortly, whan the sonne was to reste,
> So hadde I spoken with hem everichon
> That I was of hir felaweshipe anon . . .
>
> (30–32)

We gather that Chaucer was a sociable pilgrim; his previous comments
on the accommodation at the Tabard indicate that he appreciated comfort as well as convivial company, both of which were very necessary to
travellers in the middle ages. His 'ful devout corage' (line 22) in no way
makes him ill at ease in this world. The modest way in which he offers to
describe the company adds a further detail to the unselfconscious self-
portrayal of an unaffected and affable fellow—a good companion.

We do not have to read very far into the description of the Prioress
(118-62) to realise that, however uncomplicated and impressionable
Chaucer the pilgrim may be, Chaucer the poet is easily able to convey
to us discriminations about the other pilgrims that would appear to be
quite beyond the easy-going fellow who made himself a member of
their company. Chaucer the pilgrim is impressed by the Prioress's good
manners; Chaucer the poet makes us aware of how her charity is chiefly
directed toward her own dogs, and of how confused is the nature of that
Love which, for the Prioress, conquers all (162). At the very outset of the
portrait of the Monk, our suspicions of Chaucer are further aroused.
We are told that the Monk 'loved venerie' (which normally means
hunting) and in the next line (167) that he was 'a manly man', which
suggests the other meaning of *venerie* (the pursuits of Venus, the classical
goddess of love). The rest of the line seriously suggests, as if it were the
most natural thing in the world, that the Monk would make a good
abbot. Chaucer the pilgrim might think that manliness qualified a
monk to be an abbot—not so Chaucer the poet. The poet is clearly
having a joke with us—at the expense of the celibacy of contemporary
monks, but also at the expense of the simplicity of his narrator, the
pilgrim named Chaucer. Immediately afterwards we hear that the bells
on the Monk's bridle rang 'als cleere/And eek as loude, as dooth the
chapel belle'. We already know that the Monk (who is vowed to poverty)
has many horses and is fond of hunting (a common gibe against monks,
who owned plenty of land to hunt over). This last line insinuates, once
again in a comically unexpected way, that the Monk obeyed the sum-
mons of the hunt more promptly than that of the chapel. It is clear that
the pilgrim narrator is unconscious of this irony, and that the straightfaced poet is enjoying his little joke. This double perspective persists

throughout the *Prologue*. The pleasant sociability of the pilgrim Chaucer may well have been part of Chaucer's own character; social ease is part of the diplomat's life. But the impressionability of the narrator is less likely to have been so prominent a feature of a retired Customs officer. It is unavoidable that we become conscious of the narrator as a character distinct from the poet. The man in the poem is not the same as the man who wrote the poem and read it to the court. This was first pointed out by E.T. Donaldson, but it must have been sensed by all those readers who have enjoyed Chaucer's irony.* It follows that we do not always accept the opinion of the narrator on the other pilgrims, nearly all of whom impress him hugely. The gallery of portraits is thus viewed from two angles simultaneously—the social surface of every character, as disclosed to the narrator's innocent eye, and something of each pilgrim's inner nature also.

The gullible narrator is a common figure in fiction—as in Swift's *Gulliver's Travels* (1726), or Dickens's *Pickwick Papers* (1837). But he was especially common in the dream-vision poems so prominent in the narrative literature of the thirteenth and fourteenth centuries. Two of the poems Chaucer imitated, the French *Romance of the Rose* and Dante's *Divine Comedy*, were dream-visions in which the dreamer is ignorant and has to be instructed by the figures he meets in his dream, and particularly by his guide. Three of the greatest English poems of Chaucer's day were dream-visions also: Langland's *Piers Plowman*, Gower's *Confessio Amantis* and the anonymous *Pearl*. Chaucer translated the *Roman de la Rose*; all his longer poems before the *Tales*, except for *Troilus and Criseyde*, are dream-visions. Chaucer often makes himself a broadly comic figure in these early poems, and is always having a joke with the audience in that conspiratorial way which is so characteristically English. There was, then, nothing surprising in the idea of Chaucer asking us to laugh at him as well as with him. In the language of the comic stage, Chaucer the pilgrim is the 'straight man' who allows the people he meets to do all the talking—and to give themselves away in the process.

A frequent feature of the dream-vision was that the dreamer met at the outset a number of personified abstractions whose portraits are given in series. That is how the *Romance of the Rose* begins, and J.V. Cunningham has pointed out that the *General Prlogue* is an adaptation of this useful expository device into a more realistic mode† Chaucer's adaptation has been so successful that the origins of the device of the dreamer in the portrait-gallery have been forgotten.

*E.T. Donaldson, *Speaking of Chaucer*, Athlone Press, London, 1970, pp. 1–12.

†J.V. Cunningham, 'Convention as Structure—The *Prologue* to *The Canterbury Tales*', in *Geoffrey Chaucer: A Critical Anthology*, edited by J.A. Burrow, Penguin Books, Harmondsworth, 1969, pp. 218–32.

The final section of the *Prologue*, in which the pilgrims accept the Host's proposal of a tale-telling game, in which he is to be the judge, is also illuminated by this parallel with the dream-vision. The Host becomes the pilgrims' guide, and all the pilgrims agree to obey him. Like the guides in Chaucer's early poems, the Host is a manipulator—talkative, uncontrollable and slightly mischievous. As master of the game, he is not altogether a suitable figure to preside over a pilgrimage: he drinks and swears, and teases and bullies the less important pilgrims, notably Chaucer himself. Rather like Falstaff at the end of Shakespeare's *Henry IV*, he overdoes things and has to be snubbed at the end, in this case by the Parson. A richly comic character, the Host plays many roles in the pilgrimage.

The original audience, however, would have noticed that the innocent narrator's confidence was very easily won by the Host, and would also have been familiar with stories where a rash promise (such as all the pilgrims make to obey the Host) turns out alarmingly. The Host is a jolly character, and has often been seen as the incarnation of Merrie England. He does indeed turn the pilgrimage into a merry game, a rather mad game, but by the same token we must expect such a figure to be dethroned at the end—as the Lord of Misrule was in medieval comic plays. Indeed the Pardoner, an expert on drinking, describes the tavern as the devil's temple. But he was sitting in a pub at the time, and is later exposed as a fake by the Host himself. It would be a grave mistake to see the Host as a figure of the Devil—after all, Chaucer's family had made their living by selling drink—but it would also be a mistake to take him, or any of the pilgrims, as Chaucer the pilgrim does, entirely at their face value.

The portraits

While it is necessary to consider the portraits of the pilgrims in context, and to remember that they are seen through the innocent eyes of the narrator, any critical comment on the *Prologue* must chiefly concentrate on the portraits themselves. First to be considered is the order of appearance, which might be set out as follows:

(1) Military: Knight (35 lines), Squire (21), Yeoman (16).
(2) Clergy: Prioress (44), Monk (43), Friar (61).
(3) Bourgeois: Merchant (14), Clerk (23), Sergeant of the Law (21), Franklin (29), Guildsmen (18), Cook (8), Shipman (22), Doctor of Physic (33), Wife of Bath (31).
(4) Good Men: Parson (51), Ploughman (12).
(5) Petty Bourgeois: Miller (21), Manciple (19), Reeve (35).
(6) Church Officers: Summoner (45), Pardoner (45).

Medieval social theory divided the King's subjects into three Estates: the Military, the Clergy and the Laity. Chaucer observes this division, although the Clerk and Parson are included with the Laity. The Laity—groups (3), (4) and (5)—are arranged in only a rough order of precedence, unlike the first two Estates. The Sergeant of the Law, for example, would outrank the two men introduced before him; and the Franklin, as an old established landholder, would outrank the newly rich Sergeant. These, however, are minor details. The Laity are divided into three groups here: the financially independent upper-middle class, and the lower-middle class who work for them; with, between the two, the Parson and Ploughman, free men who belong with the gentle classes but, because of their honesty, are poorer than their social inferiors. Finally, we have the ecclesiastical villains.

As a panorama of medieval life—a thing it was not primarily supposed to be (see page 46)—the pilgrimage excludes the top and bottom of society, and also women, with the exception of a Prioress with her attendant nuns, and an independent widow. It is striking that everyone in groups (3), (5) and (6) is more or less motivated by avarice, with the exception of the Clerk, who stands in stark contrast between the Merchant and the Sergeant. The Military are exempt from this bourgeois vice, and so are the senior Clergy, with the exception of the Friar, though both the conventual religious are too worldly for their profession.

The Military

Knights had dominated English society since the Norman Conquest, and it is significant that Chaucer begins his catalogue with so shining an example of Christian chivalry, thus setting an ideal standard, of which nearly all the other pilgrims fall short. The Knight is defined in terms of his virtues (45-6) and actions (he has lived in the saddle as a defender of the faith), rather than by his appearance and words. The Knight is also distinguished from his son, who has fought against fellow-Christians in France, whereas the Knight's heroism is religious in impulse. In his courtesy to all and his modesty of dress he completes the figure of the English Christian gentleman, and is one of three pilgrims who are presented as perfect. Like the Parson and the Ploughman, the thrice-worthy Knight is the ideal of his Estate.

All the pilgrims are described in terms of superlatives: each is the perfect example of his or her type. The Knight is the antique pattern of the chivalry of Edward III's time; his son is a type of gallant young lover, fresh and fashionable, perhaps like some members of Chaucer's court audience. His description is an example of the principle of contrast which governs much of the arrangement of the *Prologue*, even down to apparently casual detail. The Knight had good horses but was not gay in appearance himself (74); indeed his coarse tunic is all rusty. His son is dressed up like a picture of the Spring; he cuts a fine figure on a horse (94), but no horse is mentioned. The father fights in his lord's war, and has thrice slain his foe; for his part, the son has done well for a beginner in his *chyvachie* across the Channel, in the hope of gaining his *lady*'s favour. (We must bear in mind that the Black Prince, Edward III's son and Richard II's father, had led the English army into battle at the age of fifteen; and that Chaucer himself had been a French prisoner-of-war by the time he was twenty.) The Squire's prowess is as a lover rather than as a knight: like the birds of lines 9–11, he does not sleep at night. However, though he is treated with some amusement, the Squire is a delightful figure; Chaucer's attitude seems indulgent rather than censorious, not unlike that of Duke Theseus in the *Knight's Tale* towards the young lovers Palamon and Arcite: Theseus remembers that he was a lover himself when young. Besides, the Squire is a dutiful son.

The Yeoman's portrait is perhaps the most vivid in the *Prologue*, yet it is entirely anonymous. In keeping with medieval admiration for professional skill, the adverb Chaucer chooses to describe the way the Yeoman looked after his *takel* is 'yeomanlike'. He is every inch an archer and a forester, resplendent in the badges of his trade. The archers in the English army were instrumental in winning the battles of the Hundred Years War (1337–1453). The Knight and his follower are thus an emblem of the great English past.

The Clergy

The clerical Estate presents a much less worthy trio. The Prioress is a lady to her fingertips; as for the Monk, 'he was a lord ful fat and in good poynt'; the Friar is a libertine, a playboy and a confidence trickster. They are each precisely what they should not be.

The Prioress's faults are, however, venial. Like all Prioresses in the middle ages, and some today, she has the manners of the upper class, which the narrator appears to admire greatly, describing them at length. He is also fascinated by her delicious appearance, which is that of a heroine of romance, as is her name. Her tenderness to her dogs, and the ambiguous motto on her rosary, suggest a rather more serious diversion of interest on the part of one devoted to the service of Christ. However, her tale is as conventionally pious as her manners are exquisite. The narrator is clearly bewitched by her glamorous looks and the appearance of a romantic sensibility.

Love has also conquered the other two celibates, the *manly* Monk and the *wanton* Friar. The Monk, whose name is later given as Don

John, and Friar Huberd both have love tokens, like Madame Eglen-
tyne. The Monk's gold pin with a love-knot (196–7) echoes the Nun's
gold brooch; the Friar carries a stock of pins to give to pretty women
(234). All three regular clergy have names (unlike the military trio) and
all three have love-tokens: an example of the use of significant detail to
link portraits. Both men have luxurious tastes and dress expensively.
The Friar's corruption, however, goes further than the Monk's.

Monks and nuns had been established in the Church for a thousand
years, and their shortcomings, amusingly displayed here, are those of a
worldliness and weakness that was familiar to the laity. Monks and
nuns were commonly the brothers and sisters of the lords and ladies
they too often resembled. The Friars, however, were relatively new,
and their hypocrisy was more resented, as is clear from the volume of
anti-fraternal satire from the later middle ages. With a roving commis-
sion to beg, they could pry into every household and get the better of
the housewife. The Friar's portrait is longer by ten lines than that of any
other pilgrim.

The hunting Monk is a familiar caricature and the details of his fine
horses, his fur cuffs and his fat swan could be paralleled from other
anti-clerical satire in the middle ages. It might be more profitable, then,
to focus on details of Chaucer's art rather than on his social criticism.
Three techniques used in the portrait are repeated elsewhere. Few of the
pilgrims are presented entirely by listing visual details, as in the case of
the Yeoman; the chief method, especially in satirical portraits, is to
describe with admiration and enthusiasm all those features of which
the victim himself is particularly proud. Thus the Monk's manliness,
fine horses, supple boots and diet are remarked on with warm approval.
Secondly, the narrator appears to echo the words of the pilgrim's most
characteristically revealing statements. Thus, lines 174–89 virtually
report a conversation in which the Monk gives himself away by pro-
testing against the strictness of the old Rule of St Benedict. Yet, as a
Regular, he has bound himself to keep these Rules by a religious vow.
However the pilgrim Chaucer draws further attention to the Monk's
laxity by mentioning two further monastic obligations, namely, daily
study and manual labour, and crowns the irony by asking how the
world shall be served. While the established monastic orders provided
many excellent administrators in secular fields, this was not at all the
intention of their founders, who withdrew from this world in order to
meditate on the next. By accepting the Monk's secular role and, in his
eagerness to agree, emphasising its (entirely false) premise, Chaucer's
narrator reveals his own ignorance and the Monk's stupidity.

These two techniques, praising the subject's most inappropriate
vices and quoting his idiocies with approval, are part of Chaucer's basic
satirical method, which is to allow fools to give themselves away. The

third technique—word-play—is different and less obvious, as it often relies on a knowledge of Middle English. The play on *venerie* (166) has been noticed above. Another example is *enoynt* (199): the narrator says the Monk's bald head and jolly face gleamed with good living, whereas the head was bald because it was tonsured in sign of renunciation of manly vanity, and had been anointed, not with fat living but with the sacramental oil of Holy Orders. The satire is not bitter but comical, as the Monk seems to have not the faintest understanding of the monastic ideal.

The same ironies are applied more sarcastically to the Friar. He is the most skilful seducer in all the four (celibate) orders (211). He kindly arranges marriages—for girls that he has made pregnant (212-4). He gives an easy penance—in return for a good bribe (223-4). These are examples of vice being praised. Lines 225-30 exemplify the second technique of echoing the Friar's transparent excuses. His plausible patter is again quoted in lines 243-8. There seems to be an obscene *double entendre* on the word *post* in line 214.

Two further, more poetic, features are exemplified in the portrait of the Friar. One is the use of the rhyming couplet for the purposes of comic anticlimax, as in lines 215-16:

Ful wel biloved and famulier was he
With frankeleyns over all in his contree.

The first line praises the Friar's gift of friendly intimacy and raises expectations that the object of these fraternal attentions will be the deserving poor. The second reveals that he is particularly fond of people who can entertain him luxuriously. In lines 223-4, the rhyme *penaunce/pitaunce* is particularly telling. Finally, there is a rare example of a poetic simile in lines 265-7:

And in his harpyng, when that he hadde songe
His eyen twynkled in his heed aryght
As doon the sterres in the frosty nyght.

Most of the images in the *Prologue* are proverbial; this is more decorative. However, the comparison of the charming Friar's twinkling eyes to the stars is rendered suddenly chilling by the inclusion of the adjective *frosty*. The calculating nature of the professional parasite is revealed by an irony of which the artless narrator remains unconscious. It is by these tiny touches that the poet makes his effects, and converts the objects of his satire from types into believable people. It is because the narrator portrays them so sympathetically and admiringly, for being what they are, that Chaucer is often regarded as being a humorous and comic writer rather than a reforming satirist.

The Bourgeois

After the lavish detail and display of the Friar's description, the Merchant's is short and understated. Yet every seemingly off-hand line tells us much more about this man of substance: four on his good clothes; four on his talk, boastful and fearful by turns; five on his shady financial dealing; an inconclusive final couplet.

The guileless character of the narrator is now so well established that we expect him to be impressed by anyone. He prattles on, full of empty phrases like 'ful well', 'for anything', 'For sothe'. In the last couplet he reinforces 'for sothe' with 'sooth to sey', like the most artless talker, and repeats 'worthy man' from line 279. Yet the poet artfully conveys to us that even his narrator finds the Merchant rather dull: he was *worthy* (that is, he seemed a sound man) but chose not to give his name. The Merchant may have travelled in company for safety's sake. His self-importance about his business is self-defeating, since his confidential remark to the narrator that no one knew he was in debt (280) is gossiped to the whole world. We now appreciate the force of lines 31–2:

So hadde I spoken with hem everichon
That I was of hir felaweship anon.

The Clerk's portrait is in contrast to the Merchant's, as the Squire's is to the Knight's. The Merchant is worldly, the Clerk unworldly, and this shows in every detail of their clothes, mounts, interests and conversation. The man of money booms his business; the philosopher is crisp and instructive. The portraits are linked by the word *sownynge* (275, 307).

The narrator, a man of the world, is amused by the Clerk's unworldliness, and jokes about this philosopher who has no gold. But the poet speaks warmly about his love of books, his true piety and his elevated, economical speech. The difference between the values of the poet and of his narrator is evident.

The Sergeant is another impressively learned man, but with plenty of gold in his coffer. He applies his superlative skill to personal enrichment, in further contrast to the Oxford cleric. It can be seen now that the placing of the Clerk's portrait was for reasons of dramatic and moral contrast, not of social precedence. The moral theme of greed is forced into prominence by this sandwiching of the spiritual man between the men of substance. (The lawyer is implicitly the more substantial, since he turns his fees and robes into land, which is more secure than money.)

The manner and conversation of the three men are again compared. The lawyer's words *seemed* worthy of reverence (312–3), whereas the Clerk's few words were spoken with reverence. The Clerk's wisdom is seen in the 'hy sentence' and 'moral virtue' of his speech; to judge by his words, the Sergeant seemed wise, but his expertise has brought him wariness and discretion—worldly prudence rather than wisdom. His *writyng* (326) was more reliable than his word, for his writing secured the title of his land. A distrust of lawyers shows in the use of the word *semed* (322) repeated from line 313. The simplicity of line 322 makes it as effective today as it was five hundred years ago, despite all the changes in the language.

The companion of the purchaser of land is a land-holder. The Franklin's assured social standing exempts him from the money-making that affects other pilgrims, but in his Epicureanism (see page 24) he shows the same liking for self-gratification that makes even the most wayward pilgrim so enjoyably individual. The Franklin's philosophy and style of life are picturesquely described, with poetic figures (332, 345-6, 358); the final lines list the important offices that had brought him in contact with the Sergeant.

The attractive picture of country hospitality is the first of many in English. Particularly Chaucerian is its delightful combination of cordiality, freshness, slight hyperbole and slight mockery, as in lines 349-50:

Ful many a fat partrich hadde he in muwe,
And many a breem and many a luce in stuwe.

As often in Chaucer, it is at the rhyme that the wit becomes apparent:

Whit was his berd as is a dayesye;
Of his complexioun he was sangwyn.
Wel loved he by the morwe a sop in wyn.

The simple, factual lines succeed each other without a hint of malice, yet the third line, rhyming *wyn* with *sangwyn*, suggests that the wine may have helped the blood in producing the Franklin's ruddy complexion. This kind of identical rhyme was much admired at the time. The good living of the Franklin is regarded indulgently by Chaucer, as is shown by the innocence of the comparisons to the daisy and morning milk.

The absence of a link between the Franklin and the Guildsmen contributes to the feeling that Chaucer is making an unpremeditated report on his fellow pilgrims. The Guildsmen are perhaps the least interesting members of the pilgrimage, partly because they are not individualised (none of them tells a tale) and partly because they are the object of an anti-bourgeois satire that is rather broad and predictable. The guilds, though their members were artisans, had great wealth, and were clearly able to ignore the sumptuary laws which prescribed the particular type of dress which was prescribed to be worn by each class and trade (see note to 366). Aldermen, and more especially their wives, have been an easy target for satire ever since the middle ages. Their simple pride in their wealth, and their wives' social pretensions, amuse Chaucer—as is shown in the superb hyperbole of *roialliche* in the last line, an example of the poet's intuitive understanding of the social fantasies of the worthy matrons. Another characteristic touch is the approval given by the narrator to this social pride in line 375.

The Guildsmen's own cook is a sign of their affluence. Like all the pilgrims, the Cook too is the best of his kind, and, as usual, Chaucer delights in giving us all the special language of this particular art. However, despite the narrator's enthusiasm, his dishes sound ordinary enough, compared with the fare expected of the Franklin's cook. Is the *mormal* on his shin the result of his connoisseurship of London's ale? This is the sort of question prompted by the straightfaced (repulsive) juxtaposition of the *mormal* and the *blankmanger*. As with Franklin's *sangwyn* complexion, we cannot always be sure, but that Chaucer enjoyed such urbane ironies is certain. His background would also have given him a thorough knowledge of the catering trade.

The same inside knowledge informs the portrait of the Shipman. The first eight lines give us a picturesque sailor, suntanned, comically unfamiliar with horses. The tenth contains a wonderfully unexpected climax:

Ful many a draughte of wyn had he ydrawe
Fro Burdeux-ward, whil that the chapman sleep.

The sentence is innocent until the last two words deliver the sting in its tail. Perhaps the vintner's son is repaying a grudge. We now hear of the Shipman's method of dealing with captives, and the dagger of lines 392-3 begins to look more dangerous. The vivid glimpse of the Shipman's villainy rapidly fades, however, under the lengthy catalogue of his impressive professional skills, ending in a circumstantial point added as an afterthought, like the comment on the Cook's ability with blankmanger. Such details allow us to believe that Chaucer is recalling what the man had told him.

The theme of food and drink, raised with the Prioress and the Monk and then dominating the portrait of the Franklin, continues with the Doctor of Physic. First, however, we hear of his professional prowess— the most pedantically encyclopedic of all these catalogues. Like the Knight, he is a 'verray, parfit' example of his kind, but in his case this involves conspiracy with the apothecary against the patient—an ancient complaint against doctors. After he has displayed to us his improbably vast Arabic knowledge, we come to his diet. As we might expect from the best doctor in the world (412), he eats moderately, not excessively:

> Dut of grcct norissyng and digcstiblc.
> His studie was but litel on the Bible.

The description moves immediately to his (costly) dress, but the one-line sentence about the Doctor's neglect of the Bible is a shrewd thrust, as unexpected as the Shipman's nocturnal thieving. The rhyme is particularly clever, pointedly contrasting the Doctor's scrupulous and learned care for his body with his neglect of his soul. The last two couplets destroy the Doctor's character: to him the Black Death has brought gold, gold which he is not going to pass on to others. Meanness was an even more unpopular vice in the middle ages than it is now. The impressive edifice is inhabited by a miser.

The liveliness of the Wife of Bath, Chaucer's most famous character, comes as a relief. Her portrait here is enormously amplified by the long preamble to her tale, where she indulges in unrestrained autobiography. Her garrulous tongue is only hinted at in line 474. In her *Prologue* she explains her five husbands, and also two apparently inconsequential points of the portrait—her deafness (446) and the connection between her wandering and her teeth (467-8). The illogic of the narrator's *but* in line 446 is characteristic of him—she was a good woman but unfortunately rather deaf. The deafness, however, is not an insignificant detail, but the result of a blow on the ear from her fifth husband. He had been reading to her from an encyclopedic work on the faults of women, when she knocked him into the fire and tore three leaves from his book; he struck her on the ear, but was so alarmed when she fainted that she was able to make him promise to give her sovereignty in the marriage. In medieval theory and law, biblical in origin, the man is the head of the woman, and should be obeyed. The Wife, however, is not receptive to this doctrine, and her deafness is symbolic of this unwillingness to listen. Physical characteristics often have moral significance in the portraits. Thus the Wife explains in her *Prologue* (603):

> Gat-tothed I was, and that bicam me weel;
> I hadde the prente of seinte Venus seel.

(I was gate-toothed, which became me well; I had the print of St Venus's seal.) Medieval students of physiology held that to have teeth widely spaced (gate-toothed) was a sign of boldness, falseness, gluttony and lasciviousness; the Wife, who was born under Venus (who was no Saint), regards it as confirming her venereal nature. This explains why the Wife's 'gate' teeth gave her so many opportunities to wander off the road. It is characteristic of Chaucer that these two apparently irrelevant physical details are made to seem even more casual by being qualified by 'and that was scathe' and 'soothly for to seye'—the ultra-colloquial phrases of his chatty and light-headed narrator.

The Wife's portrait begins with an evidently standard feature of the dreadful women whom clerks (and comic writers) in the middle ages liked to caricature. She is self-important and vain (449-52) in exactly the same way as the wives of the Guildsmen (376-8). However, this liking for display is cleverly combined by Chaucer with her profession (cloth-making); and her vanity in church (a scandal to clerics) is treated with the hyperbole of *roialliche* (378), but here carried to magnificent heights of absurdity. The Church required that at Mass women should cover their heads, lest their hair distract the men. The Wife's cover-chiefs, of her own manufacture, weigh *ten pound* (or so the narrator dares swear, though he has never seen her in church on Sunday). Her stockings are scarlet and tight-laced, and her shoes are 'moyste and newe'. She is thus the scarlet woman, flaunting her wares, whom the preachers against female vanity loved to hate. But—and this is very Chaucerian—she is both sexually attractive and at the same time ridiculously over-dressed. Her face is *bold* and *red* (the colour of Mars) but also *fair* (pretty).

The Wife is thus the monster of anti-feminist satire—aggressive, nagging, gossiping, lustful, vain, wasteful, domineering and—still worse—dominant. But she is also more human than any stereotype, and some critics find her lovable in her overflowing human vanity. Above all, she is a comic figure. The touches of hyperbole at the beginning of her portrait are followed by a series of hints that her amorous adventures have been epically excessive. Apart from her five husbands and other youthful company we are told that she had 'passed many a straunge strem' and knew a lot about 'wandrynge by the weye'. These nudges and winks from Chaucer are continued in the details of her easy riding, her spurs, and finally:

Of remedies of love she knew per chaunce
For she koude of that art the olde daunce.

This couplet may not be obscene, but the *remedies* and *olde daunce* cannot be construed as compliments to the Wife's virtue.

A last point about the Wife's portrait is that it contains several symbolic details of a sort that appears increasingly in the satirical portraits of the lower characters. Thus, the redness of her face, her hat as broad as a shield and her sharp spurs all suggest her martial qualities.

The Good Men

The Parson is 'a good man', but his goodness is of a very different kind from that of the Wife, who is introduced as 'a good wife'. The Wife is described as *worthy* because she has had five husbands; the Merchant was also *worthy*; and the Manciple is *gentil*. Yet these words have also been applied to the Knight. It is clear that we must discriminate between moral worth and social worth in the way that the narrator does not. But even he points out that the poor Parson is spiritually rich. And he refrains from calling the Parson 'a good felawe'.

The Parson and the Ploughman are truly good men, strikingly different and apart from the social world through which we have been descending. They are described in terms of their virtues rather than their physical appearance, diet or tastes. The materialists are described materialistically, the idealists idealistically. The contrast is absolute. Both brothers are characters formed directly upon the ideals of the Church and the Gospel. Unlike all the bourgeois characters, and most of the clergy, they give rather than take; they love God and their neighbour; they work hard for others; and they are humble. Although such men were as rare as saints, their ideals were accepted as normal and are clearly shared by Chaucer. There is energy as well as piety in both descriptions, and they are made persuasive by the same colloquial actuality that animates the other portraits. The Parson was 'loth to curse', he *caughte* the words out of the gospel, he *ran* not to London, his speech was not 'daungerous ne digne'. The Plowman was 'a trewe swynkere' and loved God 'thogh him gamed or smerte'. The Parson is consistently developed beyond an ideal conception into a recognisable character. He is a 'noble example', but he is also a real village priest: if his brother carts dung, the parson speaks of *a shiten shepherd*. Chaucer further applies the metaphor of *clennesse* to gold and to the mire which encumbers the sheep. Sacred allegory is thus made domestic. Above all, this unmercenary shepherd is *benign* (483, 518):

> To drawen folk to hevene by fairnesse,
> By good ensample, this was his bisynesse.

But he does not rely on his charisma nor on his dignity: without being over-scrupulous, he is prepared to snub an obstinate person sharply when necessary—as he does the Host at the end of the pilgrimage. He is a realist, beside whom the Ploughman seems more completely idealised —apart from his mare.

The Petty Bourgeois and the Church Officers

The last six pilgrims are introduced as a group. What have they in common? All except Chaucer (who includes himself as a joke) are dishonest stewards who defraud those they serve, and abuse positions of trust. They are criticised with a less friendly irony.

There was broad comedy in the portrait of the Wife of Bath, not without mild vulgarity. The Miller, however, is a grotesque figure, coarse and menacing. His description is unprecedentedly physical, partly because his brutal strength is the key to his character (he is a bully) and partly because of the satirical tradition of caricaturing low and vicious persons as gross and beastly.

His powerful physical presence is immediately suggested, and there follow sundry unattractive details of his features, with a final mixture of remarks on his habits and dress. Closer attention to the portrait, however, transforms this 'realistic' physical portrait into a complex moral emblem.

Discord is suggested by wrestling, the unhingeing and splitting of doors, the weapons he carries, his jangling (560) and the bagpipes—an inauspicious instrument with which to lead a harmonious band of pilgrims. Even the Miller's profession involves breaking and crushing. Bestial affinities are suggested by the brawn, bones, ram, sow, fox, and the sow's ears (out of which, according to the old English proverb, silk purses cannot be made). The hairs on the wart on the top of his nose are red, as are his beard and his huge mouth, whereas his nostrils are black. These last two details seem sinister, even hellish: the Devil's mouth is portrayed in medieval painting as the gaping mouth of a furnace. The Miller's thieving and his dirty mind seem quite minor beside the power and cruelty implicit in his portrait.

The Manciple, by contrast, is *gentil*, but is also a thief of others' food, like the Miller, yet more discreetly. Discretion and prudence are ironically described as *wise* in line 569 and *wisdom* in line 575. In this wise buying, the Manciple emulates the wise purchasing of the Sergeant of the Law (p.23). The pilgrim Chaucer is amused by seeing the legal defrauders legally defrauded by their uneducated servant. Indeed the irony of the portrait only becomes unmistakable with the last line. The Manciple is not individualised—he is a faceless man.

The Reeve, by contrast, is immediately described as mean in every sense of the word. He is scrawny, unlike the Miller, and angry, unlike the Manciple. In other respects he closely resembles the Manciple, whose lines 579–86 apply exactly to the Reeve: he cheats his lord in a way that the lord cannot detect. He is also like the Miller in that he oppresses those below him (603–5). Millers were the natural enemies of Reeves and of carpenters, and the Reeve is a carpenter too. This rivalry breaks out in their respective tales, and it becomes clear why they ride at opposite ends of the pilgrimage.

The three dishonest stewards are thus very closely linked by similarities and contrasts, and the hostility of Miller and Reeve prepares us for their tales, which immediately follow the Knight's and set in motion the dramatic conflicts which animate the *Tales* thereafter. However, the Reeve's portrait has rich touches beyond the necessities of any future dramas. There are few more varied passages in the *Prologue* than lines 603-12. The Reeve's professional skills become sinister in line 605, and the deathly fear in which he is held casts a deeply ironic light upon his comfortable house, the epitome, apparently, of all that is innocent and wholesome in country life. His lord's kindness to him and his cruelty to his inferiors may echo New Testament parables. But the Reeve's manipulation of his lord is Chaucer's own, particularly the Reeve's gratification in being thanked by his victim (612). Chaucer's delight in exposing hypocrisy reflects a medieval love of honesty and a Gothic taste for dramatic reversal. One of Chaucer's most famous lines is 'The smylere with the knyf under the cloke' (*Knight's Tale*, line 1998).

Finally comes the precious pair whom even the pilgrim derides as villains. The Summoner is the simpler of the two: a lecher, a drunkard, a corrupt officer of the law, easily bribed by a drink from a fellow-criminal; demanding bribes from those who prefer their purses to their souls; corrupting the young. Sarcasm rather than irony is the note, as in the comments on the Summoner's Latin (637-46) and his kindness (647-65). Lechery is his ruling passion: his face is *fyr-reed* (624) and he is *hoot* (626). This is expressed in his facial acne and his love of hot foods and strong drink. For him *wyn* rhymes with *Latyn* (638) and *concubyn* (650). Bread and wine also enter into the last couplet, and it may be that, as in the *Pardoner's Tale*, these are connected with the inability of the sinner to partake of communion. Excommunication was the ultimate penalty of the court the Summoner served.

The Pardoner is sillier and more corrupt than the cunning but stupid Summoner. He sings alto to the Summoner's bass, and it is clearly stated that he is physically a eunuch, an incomplete man (691). This effeminacy explains his affected hairstyle, and possibly his carrying the pardons or bulls in his lap, as a compensating source of potency. The narrator scorns the Pardoner's effeminacy but, as always, respects professional skill.

The Pardoner has false relics, which fool the ignorant country folk into giving him money which should go to the parish priest. He preaches so well because he knows that his takings depend upon it. This account of the Pardoner's art is drawn from his own boasting. Indeed the Pardoner's own *Prologue* and *Tale* dramatically illustrate in detail how he uses his relics, how he preaches and tells a story, and how he blackmails the guilty and ignorant into buying his pardons. The Host, however, exposes the sterile nature of the Pardoner's false bulls from Rome, and exposes him also as a eunuch. The Pardoner is contemptible because he defrauds the poor, like a crooked insurance salesman; but he is doubly contemptible on the pilgrimage, because he usurps the function of the Parson. Pardoners could not pardon anyone's sins, nor were they licensed to preach. This Pardoner was not a cleric, did not come

from Rome, sold false pardons and—worst of all, as his *Tale* shows—
did not believe in the pardons he professed to sell. He was thus a complete fraud. The theme of his sermon is, by a sublime irony, *'Radix
malorum est cupiditas'* ('the love of money is the root of all evils'). Far
from being a pilgrim, he is a dangerous parasite, a wolf in sheep's
clothing. Hence he is symbolically made a eunuch of repugnant appearance—a fit partner for the ecclesiastical policeman who aids and abets
him. However, like the Wife of Bath, the Pardoner is a character
developed much more fully in his *Prologue* and *Tale*.

From this review of the series of portraits it can be seen that *cupiditas*,
or avarice, is a dominant theme. The penitential motive for the pilgrimage, which the Parson's Tale so starkly recalls to the minds of the pilgrims, is clearly not uppermost in the minds of the Squire, the professional men, the Wife, the various dishonest stewards, or the Host.
However, only the Pardoner is there merely to make money out of the
others. The loathing felt for the vice which the Pardoner embodies
reflects a belief in the Church's genuine power of pardon. The warm
portrait of the Parson also shows that it would be wrong to imagine
Chaucer as anti-clerical. That most Catholic poet, Dante, put contemporary Popes into his *Inferno*. Chaucer detests the mercenary and loves
the shepherd (514). Toward those clerics who fall between the two—the
Nun, Monk and Friar—he is subtly, broadly or keenly satirical. He was
not a prophet of Reform, but a sincere and orthodox Christian, who
was a humorist but also a realist.

The game

The remainder of the *Prologue* reverts to the less formal texture of
Chaucer's initial narrative, and the lines before the introduction of the
Host (715-46) add nothing to the story—but much to the atmosphere.
After the dense detail of the portraits, Chaucer relaxes and re-estab-
lishes the character of his narrator as an amiable but diffident bumbler,
confiding to the audience: 'My wit is short, ye may wel understonde.'
An impenetrable humility is the poet's favourite guise.
     The Host recreates the merry cheer which was a medieval social ideal.
Having feasted the pilgrims (and received payment), he proposes a
game which will increase their mirth—and cost them nothing (668). In
fact it is to cost all but one of them the price of another supper at the
Tabard on their return. The Host, as president of the game, will be able
to play the part of 'a marchal in an halle' for which his physique and
talents fit him so well. He thus secures custom, profit, diversion and
what the Americans call an ego-trip. While we are to note the Host's
commercial shrewdness and his dexterity in stage-managing this take-

over, we are also meant to be impressed by his good humour. He cap-
tures the good will of the pilgrims by flattery and exuberance, in a
masterly blend of professional sales-talk. At the end of the pilgrimage,
had it gone according to the Host's plan, he would have had 'a thank
and yet a cote and hood', like the Manciple. Unlike the Manciple, however, he is genuinely a good fellow.

One consequence of the Host's cheery ultimatum is that the pilgrimage is transformed, without our noticing it, into a party game. The
pilgrim narrator enjoys good company, and may have no objection, but
not all the pilgrims may have been equally happy with the promise into
which they had been so innocently hustled—the Prioress, the Parson,
the Miller and the Pardoner might all have different objections. But
the Host manages it so that we hear nothing of objections, but only of
ease, mirth, merriment, disport, comfort, wine and ale. Also that anyone who disobeys him will have to pay the expenses of the others, and
that the prize supper will be at a fixed price. It is notable, however, that
in the arrangements for the competition (790–801), the tales are to be
'of aventures that whilom han bifalle'—the Host's idea of a story—but
that the prize will go to him who tells 'tales of best sentence and moost
solaas', which is quite another idea, perhaps more like the poet's own.

In all of this the Host remains something of an unknown quantity.
His original description tells us less than his behaviour, but even this
remains finally elusive. *The Canterbury Tales* has already begun to
develop on dramatic lines quite different from the static descriptions we
have passed through. Our guides, the narrator and Host, are both
slightly unpredictable.

The setting-out at dawn has great narrative verve and excitement;
perhaps the Franklin did not even have time for his 'sop in wyn'. The
manly Host leads forth his flock at a quiet pace, sternly reminds them
of their oaths of obedience, and, while the horses are watered, bids the
pilgrims draw. He politely invites the senior gentleman and lady present
to begin the draw; jokingly presses the retiring Clerk to submit himself
also to the dominion of chance; and rounds up the others.

With silky irony Chaucer suggests that the Host may have fixed the
cut so that the Knight gets the short straw. The narrator is delighted by
this fortunate turn of events, as were all the pilgrims—especially, it may
be imagined, the Host, who has thus at the outset involved the most
honoured and authoritative of the pilgrims. The Knight proves to be a
good sport, and jovially agrees to tell the first tale. The pilgrimage is
forgotten and the game has begun.

Part 4

___

Hints for study

Chaucer's language

The best advice that can be given to a student of Chaucer is to make sure that he or she understands as accurately as possible exactly what Chaucer's words mean. Without a well-informed response to the sense, there can be no sensitivity to poetic qualities in the language, nor to the poet's tone of voice. Chaucer's fresh, apt and elegant English is what makes him such a model of style. And his tone of voice gives the clue to his sense of humour, which has delighted generations of readers. The narrative can be followed in translation, but without appreciation of the poet's own tongue, all finer quality is lost. The *Prologue* was composed to be read aloud, and should be read aloud in an approximation to the prevailing pronunciation, which can be gathered from one of the several modern recordings that have been made. (Pay attention to the problem of sounding the final *-e*, which was sometimes pronounced and sometimes not in Chaucer's day. Generally, we pronounce final *-e* when it is required by the rhyme or metre, and not when it is not.)

Middle English

Historians divide English into Old, Middle and Modern English. Old English came to an end with the Norman Conquest of Anglo-Saxon England in 1066. The rulers of England then spoke French, and scholars wrote in Latin. Gradually English was accepted in the fourteenth century, and was increasingly used for literary purposes. Middle English was, however, an unstable mixture of French and various English dialects, unstandardised by established court usage or printing, and the language changed continuously until a more stable stage was reached about 1500, when Modern English conventionally begins. There is no room here for a proper introduction to Middle English nor to Chaucer's use of it. Suffice it to note that he wrote in the London dialect, that he introduced the pentameter and that he brought the French rhetorical style into English.

Here are some practical hints for reading Chaucer:

(1) Read aloud to ascertain metre, rhyme and tone of voice.
(2) Pronounce all consonants fully: for example the *K* and *h* in Knight.

(3) Consult glossaries and grammatical introductions when in any doubt as to sense or grammatical function.

(4) Do not assume that a word means what it means today (for example: *lustful* zestful; *coy* quiet; *lewed* ignorant; *girl* young of either sex; *person* parson; *verray* true; *catel* property; *smal* slender; *wife* woman; *wood* mad). It is particularly important to understand the concepts of charity, truth and chivalry in their medieval senses.

(5) Make lists of common words used by the narrator in more than one sense (such as *worthy, wys, gentil, nyce, semely*) and decide on the exact sense in each instance.

(6) Write your own accurate prose translation of as much of the *Prologue* as you can.

Background

In general, follow the indications given in your edition and, in Part 5, the suggestions for further reading. Make sure you understand the exact role in society played by each pilgrim. Three subjects often give trouble:

1. *Clergy*. Distinguish between the secular clergy, like the Parson, who live in the world (either in major orders—bishop, priest, deacon—or 'clerks' in minor orders) and the regular clergy. Regulars bound themselves by a communal rule: monks, nuns, canons and friars are all regulars. However, a regular can also be a priest—like Chaucer's Friar and perhaps his Monk. Further, the Friar, though a regular, lived in the world as well as belonging to a community. The Summoner and Pardoner may or may not have been clerks. The Knight was probably also a member of a religious military order, such as the Templars or Hospitallers, or the Teutonic Knights.

2. *Penance*. For an understanding of Christianity, a knowledge of the New Testament is indispensable, and a history of medieval Christendom would be useful. Central to the *Tales* is the sacrament of penance or confession. Only God can forgive sins, but priests inherit from the apostles the power to absolve (or *shrive*) the sinner who truly repents and performs the penance imposed. The Pardoner deals only in certificates of remission of this penance or punishment, and cannot absolve sinners of their guilt. This is a crucial distinction.

3. *Hierarchy*. Medieval society was vertically organised in pyramid-style, with King and Pope at the heads of State and Church. The order of precedence is followed by Chaucer, though informally and with some exceptions. Notice the size and miscellaneous character of the bourgeois group, the majority, who had no established place in medieval social theory, which was based upon agriculture, the feudal land-

holding system and military service rather than upon commerce. Chaucer treats the middle-class values of these new men with some scorn.

Literary form

(1) Distinguish Chaucer the poet from Chaucer the pilgrim, who is a character in the poem and also its narrator.

(2) Identify the points at which the pilgrim and the poet are furthest apart, and how this difference is used for purposes of irony (notably in the portraits of the regular clergy and the richer bourgeois).

(3) Consider the effect of the Introduction and the Game upon the Portraits, and the possible relevance of the conventions of the Dream-Vision.

(4) How far do portraits of the pilgrims portray ideal types rather than real individuals? How far is the purpose of the *Prologue* moral rather than sociological? How far are the portraits informed by Chaucer's career experience, how far by his ideals, and how far by satirical convention?

(5) Notice how some pilgrims are characterised by their dress, others by their ideals; some by their physique and diet, others by their speech; some by their actions, others by their manners; some by their history, others by their tastes; all by their profession, its skills and abuses. Which pilgrims does the pilgrim Chaucer like and dislike? What do his preferences suggest about his values? How do these differ from the poet's?

(6) What are the themes which emerge from the *Prologue*? Which human qualities and weaknesses does Chaucer emphasise? Is his attitude to the weaknesses one of indignation, irony, amusement, neutrality, indulgence or approval?

(7) Consider the role of contrast in the arrangement of the portraits, and the use of significant detail to link together groups of similar pilgrims.

Questions and sample answers

Question: What is Chaucer's purpose in the *General Prologue*?

(1) To provide an introduction to the *Tales* as a whole, introducing the *tellers*, through their portraits, and the tale-telling *game*.

(2) The idealised opening and the realistic scene at the Tabard Inn immediately involve us in an attractive *narrative* that we wish to follow—an interest further stimulated by the lively portraits of the pilgrims.

(3) Chaucer also introduces himself, as a rather naïve and impressionable pilgrim; and the Host, the master of ceremonies. These two
figures are to *control the narrative* in the links between the tales.

(4) The portraits are contrasted in such a way as to suggest that certain
themes will be important, for example avarice and unworldliness;
professional skill and the end to which it is put; food and drink;
the pilgrimage itself; sexual comedy.

(5) So the *Prologue* is both an attractive, self-contained opening to a
realistic story and also an introduction to a flexible, complex and
varied work, in which several themes are already prominent.

Question: What conclusions can be drawn from the portraits in the
Prologue about Chaucer's view of medieval society?

---

(1) It was not Chaucer's purpose to present an analysis of society for
the modern historian, but to introduce a work of fiction.

(2) The portraits of the pilgrims are presented through the medium of a
very impressionable narrator, whose values do not always represent
those of the author. For example, the pilgrim Chaucer agrees that
the Monk is right to do no work (186–8), but the poet makes us doubt
the truth of this. Thus Chaucer's view is not always easy to ascertain.

(3) However, it is clear that Chaucer admires the Knight, Parson,
Ploughman and Clerk, but not the Summoner or Pardoner. His attitude to the pilgrims in between varies from indulgence (the Squire),
to irony (the Doctor) and satire (the Friar).

(4) The gallery of portraits excluded the top and bottom of society, but
it is organised in a descending order of virtue and status. The largest
group is the middle class, whose acquisitiveness is viewed with irony.
So it seems Chaucer's views were rather traditional, both morally
and socially: he disliked the avaricious and the newly-rich. Such
views are not surprising in a court poet.

(5) The portraits confirm what we know from history about the rise of
the bourgeoisie and the worldliness of the clergy. The sharpness and
shrewdness of Chaucer's views are more striking than their novelty
or historical value.

Question: Translate accurately into modern English one of the portraits and add comments.

A translation of lines 331-60: the Franklin:

In his company was a Franklin. His beard was as white as a daisy; he was sanguine of complexion. In the morning he dearly loved a cake dipped in wine. Always to live in pleasure was his settled habit, for he was a true son of Epicurus, who held the view that pleasure unalloyed was true and perfect happiness. He was a householder, and a great one: in his part of the world he was St Julian. His bread and his ale were always of the same quality; and nowhere was there a man with a better cellar. His house was never without baked dishes of fish and flesh, and they were in such plenty that in his house it snowed meat and drink, and in all conceivable delicacies. He changed his diet and his table according to the various seasons of the year. He had a great many fat partridges in coops, and many a bream and many a pike in ponds. It was a bad day for his cook if his sauce was not piquant and sharp, or if his equipment was not ready. There was always a table, covered and set, standing in his hall all day long. At the Quarter Sessions he was lord and master and sat many times as Knight of the Shire. A dagger and a purse made all of white silk as white as morning milk hung from his belt. He had been a sheriff and an auditor. Nowhere was there such a splendid landholder.

(1) The Franklin was a landholder of considerable social importance in the county as suggested by the offices he held and also by the friendship of the Sergeant of the Law.

(2) Chaucer's Franklin is not just a hospitable country gentleman (St Julian). He is also an epicure, whose extravagant and delicious food is principally there for his own pleasure (*delit*).

(3) The portrait has several picturesque and poetic touches, such as the rhyme *sangwyn/wyn* and the hyperbole of *snewed.* This makes the pilgrim both attractive and at the same time a caricature. This subtle and engaging combination of qualities is typical of Chaucer's shrewd grasp of realities, and his humanity.

Style

If *The Canterbury Tales* were written today the *Prologue* would be in prose, although some of the *Tales* require an elevated and ritual style and could not have been written in prose. Chaucer's prose was, however, rudimentary compared with his verse (see the *Tale of Melibee*).

The *Prologue* is written in rhyming pentameters and in a flexible style, basically simple and colloquial, for it is spoken aloud by the poet to his audience and purports to record his actual experience. Normally it avoids the elevation and use of imagery and allusion which are sometimes thought poetic, although the opening is elaborate and formal and there is the occasional telling use of simile later.

The language is clear, rapid, almost transparent. It draws no attention to itself except when the narrator apologises for his inadequacies or uses unusually excessive padding (such as 'for the nonys' and 'soothly for to seye'). Chaucer's expository style in the *General Prologue* is recognised as a model of simplicity and unaffected unselfconscious elegance: it gives the illusion of a varied stream of discourse, lively, free from pedantry, vulgarity or artifice. Although so ancient, it seems fresh, even naïve at times; this quaintness is the result of unfamiliarity, for although Chaucer is engaging and can be captivating, he was a civilised, courtly and urbane writer. If his age was simpler in its spirit and technology, it was sophisticated as well as earthy. Indeed, a naïve customs officer is a contradiction in terms: the naïvety of the narrator is a deliberate Chaucerian creation.

If the style is sometimes off-hand ('For blankmanger, that maad he with the beste'—387), this is partly because of the intimacy of Chaucer with his audience, his broad popularity and sanity, and partly a rhetorical skill. If art is to conceal art, Chaucer's art is to profess artlessness. Many of the casual reflections of his narrator are of a deadly accuracy:

    And yet he seemed bisier than he was.   (322)

 or But sooth to seyn, I noot how men him calle.   (284)

 or His hors were goode, but he was not gay.   (74)

 or They were adrad of hym as of the deeth.   (605)

The strength of this style lies in its confident ability to do whatever is required of it. This case reflects a solidarity with his public that no subsequent author has exceeded: Chaucer was both a sophisticated and a popular writer, as was Shakespeare, but his language is less extravagant than Shakespeare's, perhaps because his social base is broader and better integrated.

The most easily isolated poetic quality of the *Prologue* is the crispness of the rhymes. This is most obvious in the self-contained couplet:

    He was not pale as a forpyned goost:
    A fat swan loved he best of any roost.
                    (205–6)

where the association of the rhyme-words is quite unexpected, and a comic contrast is made. Or the couplet can be open:

> She was so charitable and so pitous
> She wolde wepe, if that she saugh a mous
> Kaught in a trappe . . .
>
> (143-4)

Where *mous* defines the Nun's pity as sentimentally directed towards animals, rather than towards people as 'charity' had suggested. Many of the best rhymes are for the purposes of bathos or ironic wit, reversing the expectations of the previous line. Particularly audacious are *digestible/Bible* (437-8), *Bathe/scathe* (445-6), *cloystre/oystre* (181-2), *hoot/goot* (687-8) and *bledde/fedde/deed/breed* (145-9). Each rhyme is a comment, witty and fantastic but never wild. The element of hyperbole, seen in many of the images of food, dress or physique, also appears in the spectacular skill with which Chaucer sometimes divides a couplet between two utterly disconnected subjects (and so connects them). This is seen at the end of one portrait and the beginning of the next, as at lines 207-8, 269-70 and 387-8; or in the concluding rhyme of many portraits. It is at the rhymes that we feel the sharpness that plays beneath Chaucer's easy tone.

Finally, when writing about the *Prologue*'s style or themes, its structure or social satire, take care always to quote. Quote the significant detail, the telling line or even the single word, such as *frosty* (268) or *roialliche* (378). All generalisations about the *General Prologue*, and especially about Chaucer's attitude to society, sound heavy and dull compared with the lightness of his own words.

Part 5

Suggestions for further reading

The text

The Works of Geoffrey Chaucer, edited by F.N. Robinson, second edition, Oxford University Press, London, 1957. This is still the standard edition of Chaucer's complete works and has good introductions and notes, but a limited glossary. On-the-page glossing is provided in *The Canterbury Tales*, edited by A.C. Cawley, Dent, London, 1958. There are many editions of *The Canterbury Tales*, complete and selected, and of individual tales and groups of tales, published by Harrap, Cambridge University Press and Oxford University Press.

The General Prologue, edited by P. Hodgson, Athlone Press, London, 1963

Chaucer's Canterbury Tales: The Prologue, edited by A.W. Pollard, Macmillan, London, 1903

Introductory general works

BREWER, D.S.: *Chaucer in his Time*, Nelson, London, 1963

BREWER, D.S.: *Chaucer*, third edition, Longman, London, 1973

COGHILL, N.: *The Poet Chaucer*, second edition, Oxford University Press, London, 1967

CHESTERTON, G.K.: *Chaucer*, Faber and Faber, London, 1932

ROWLAND, BERYL (ED.): *Companion to Chaucer Studies*, Oxford University Press, London, 1968

Criticism

BOWDEN, M.A.: *A Commentary on the General Prologue to the Canterbury Tales*, Macmillan, London, 1948

BRONSON, B.H.: *In Search of Chaucer*, University of Toronto Press, Toronto, 1960

BURROW, J.A. (ED.): *Geoffrey Chaucer: A Critical Anthology*, Penguin, Harmondsworth, 1969

DONALDSON, E.T.: *Speaking of Chaucer*, Athlone Press, London, 1970

The author of these notes

MICHAEL ALEXANDER was educated at Trinity College, Oxford. He has worked in publishing and universities in England and America, but since 1969 has been at the University of Stirling in Scotland, where he is a Senior Lecturer in English. His publications include *Twelve Poems*; *The Earliest English Poems* and *Beowulf* (verse translations of Old English poetry in the Penguin Classics series); and *Old English Riddles from the Exeter Book*. Critical writings include *The Poetic Achievement of Ezra Pound* (1979), *History of Old English Literature* (1983), and the volume in the York Notes series on Chaucer's *Knight's Tale*.

The first 200 titles

Series number

BEN JONSON	*The Alchemist*	(102)
	Volpone	(15)
RUDYARD KIPLING	*Kim*	(114)
D. H. LAWRENCE	*Sons and Lovers*	(24)
	The Rainbow	(59)
	Women in Love	(143)
HARPER LEE	*To Kill a Mocking-Bird*	(125)
CAMARA LAYE	*L'Enfant Noir*	(191)
LAURIE LEE	*Cider with Rosie*	(186)
THOMAS MANN	*Tonio Kröger*	(168)
CHRISTOPHER MARLOWE	*Doctor Faustus*	(127)
	Edward II	(166)
SOMERSET MAUGHAM	*Of Human Bondage*	(185)
	Selected Short Stories	(38)
HERMAN MELVILLE	*Billy Budd*	(10)
	Moby Dick	(126)
ARTHUR MILLER	*Death of a Salesman*	(32)
	The Crucible	(3)
JOHN MILTON	*Paradise Lost I & II*	(94)
	Paradise Lost IV & IX	(87)
	Selected Poems	(177)
V. S. NAIPAUL	*A House for Mr Biswas*	(180)
SEAN O'CASEY	*Juno and the Paycock*	(112)
	The Shadow of a Gunman	(200)
GABRIEL OKARA	*The Voice*	(157)
EUGENE O'NEILL	*Mourning Becomes Electra*	(130)
GEORGE ORWELL	*Animal Farm*	(37)
	Nineteen Eighty-four	(67)
JOHN OSBORNE	*Look Back in Anger*	(128)
HAROLD PINTER	*The Birthday Party*	(25)
	The Caretaker	(106)
ALEXANDER POPE	*Selected Poems*	(194)
THOMAS PYNCHON	*The Crying of Lot 49*	(148)
SIR WALTER SCOTT	*Ivanhoe*	(58)
	Quentin Durward	(54)
	The Heart of Midlothian	(141)
	Waverley	(122)
PETER SHAFFER	*The Royal Hunt of the Sun*	(170)
WILLIAM SHAKESPEARE	*A Midsummer Night's Dream*	(26)
	Antony and Cleopatra	(82)
	As You Like It	(108)
	Coriolanus	(35)
	Cymbeline	(93)
	Hamlet	(84)
	Henry IV Part I	(83)
	Henry IV Part II	(140)
	Henry V	(40)
	Julius Caesar	(13)
	King Lear	(18)
	Love's Labour's Lost	(72)
	Macbeth	(4)
	Measure for Measure	(33)
	Much Ado About Nothing	(73)